HASOR

My Soul's Journey Through Some Of My Past Lives

Based Upon True Lives

HASOR

<u>*via*</u>

April Crawford

Title: **HASOR**

My Soul's Journey Through Some Of My Past Lives

Based Upon True Lives

Authors: HASOR, April Crawford

Publisher: Connecting Wave
2629 Foothill Blvd.
Unit # 353
La Crescenta, CA 91214
www.ConnectingWave.com

ISBN-13: 978-0692568095
ISBN-10: 0692568093

For Author Information:
www.AprilCrawford.com

For other books via April Crawford:
www.AprilCrawfordBooks.com

Book Design: Allen Crawford

For Permissions: Publisher@ConnectingWave.com

Session Date: 9-27-15

Oversoul

"The moment flows in all places. Scenery may change, items of interest may alter, while the breeze gently caresses your cheek. All these things of experience allow energy to circle within, while witnessing to the outward expansion.

Tis easy to get caught up in that wind. To become engrossed in a single moment, while forgetting all others in the queue.

Each path similar with different players leading right back to the start point. How often have we circled endlessly living pointless, being pointless, while searching for conclusion?

Our incarnate moments helpful, but somewhat confusing. Often missing the lesson, while being so hungry for truth. We know these things as we move from life to life, death to death, resurrection to resurrection. Only surviving through the intervention of those further down the path. Those who can untangle the mysteries, while guiding unconditionally.

We have experienced these precious wise ones who have evolved before us. Searching for a balance, we expand in spite of our errors and failures. Held closely by those who guided us through it all.

Now our time to lead is upon us. All that has transpired to now will be useful as we extend to those who now stand in the doorway of experience.

Gladly we step forward, anxious to meet our pupil. The soul reaches out as we whisper greetings of welcome. Now it is our turn to describe the union. The new soul seeks guidance, reassurance, and a sense of knowledge.

We eagerly await the arrival of the soul and its aspects. The breeze of creation is present and we feel the vibration.

To speak of the process is our desire, to define this participation.

HASOR

We are now an Oversoul.

We are HASOR.

We speak to give understanding. We guide as those who guided us on our journey through incarnations.

The soul blends into the tapestry to begin weaving aspects of itself. Each of those aspects are valid representations of its internal reflections. A magnificent journey begins as the cry of newborn child stakes its claim upon a life. A precious life always to be remembered and honored.

We, HASOR, feel the beauty as the tapestry unfolds. This soul wishes to experience the feminine in all of its probabilities, hoping to find strength and balance in a mismatched patriarchal reality.

It should present great opportunity for growth. Our focus is to keep each aspect focused upon the goal of growth.

We shall advise as needed. Guide continuously, and love unconditionally.

So it begins....."

~HASOR

Introduction

This intent of this book is to provoke thought and to relate stories about actual "past" lives, more accurately described as "multiple lives", from the points of view of those that lived them and from certain perspectives, like you, are still living them. This includes their personal stories, including the narratives, all of which they physically write, as well as occasional observations and perspective of their, in this case, shared Oversoul.

This is all possible as they as individuals are able to assume the physical form of a rather rare Full Body Open Deep Trance Channel named April Crawford.

April Crawford has not written any of this book whatsoever. All of the chapters, including the "narrator pieces", were written by one of the multiple lives of Hasor, or by the Oversoul, HASOR.

April Crawford has the natural ability to not only allow many from the "Other Side" to speak in full two-way interactive conversation, and not only to be regressed almost instantly into her own "past" lives, but uniquely, into the "past," "future", and parallel lives *of others*.

Although this ability is not offered to telephone clients, there are some regular in-person clients and research and investment partners who have been able to participate and actually talk, in two-way fully interactive conversations with their own "past", "future", and/or parallel lives. Very interesting. Often very intense.

I mention this primarily because the level of detail that follows may seem quite unlikely, if not impossible, to some, yet it is quite common, even routine in our work, particularly in my personal in-person sessions.

The remainder of this introduction should be skipped by those who just want to get into the stories. What follows in this introduction is for those [like me] that are interested in some of the mechanics of how this book was written:

HASOR

Note that all of the chapters in this book were written in first, final, and only draft by several aspects and incarnated personalities of the incarnated Hasor, each from, and within, their own present moment perspectives as independent but connected individuals. The Oversoul, HASOR, has also added observation and comments from that Oversoul's perspective.

Some of the chapters were intentionally physically written out of book order, and then arranged later for this book by both Hasor and HASOR, for their own reasons. (Possibly to subtly, or not so subtly emphasize and remind us, me included (even though I have been talking with various nonphysical beings for many years), that time is an illusion, and/or simply, that "Time is a curious thing.")

The following chapter lengths generally reflect each of the individual open deep trance channeling sessions that allowed Hasor, her multiple lives and aspects, and her Oversoul, to completely assume the physical form of the channel necessary to write about these true lives. Do not be concerned about the channel. She was having quite amazing out of body adventures on her own during these writing sessions.

The actual session dates, where available, were left at the head of each chapter for those interested in the mechanics of such things. When you note the "time" that this book took to complete, note also that neither Hasor, nor any of them, ever lost track of where they wanted to be, even though the writing sessions were interrupted by two intervening published books, my personal sessions, several hundred *"Inner Whispers"* newsletters, and literally at least 5,000 live client sessions conducted by the Causal Plane Entity VERONICA with individuals and small groups from most countries around the world.

This book is NOT the result of what is generally known as "automatic writing". It was written directly, physically, and could have been dictated by voice if desired.

I, Allen, have visited and talked with an aspect of Hasor, in real-time two-way fully interactive conversations, in-person. That Hasor and her aspects agreed to write in long hand, but this book could have been dictated if they insisted.

For current timeframe references, some names of people, places, and businesses may have been changed to protect privacy (some at my request) or for the purposes of literary license.

Note: When I [Allen] asked if she used any "literary license", Hasor (Not the Oversoul HASOR) turned her head, looked me in the eye, and coyly, and seductively, as is this particular aspect's way, asked me, "Do you need a license to write a book here?"

Each aspect who participated in telling their story, is an individual with individual, but in this case related, multiple physical lives. Each with an Oversoul..... as are you (unless you are a first time incarnate, or have chosen in-between lives not to incarnate again, which is totally your individual choice, as it is everyone's).

~Allen, Facilitator for April Crawford

Session Date: 10-21-14

~1~

Oversoul Perspective

The silence of the eternal wraps its arm about my energy, offering a calmness of perspective. Having reached this level of awareness, my thoughts begin creating a pleasurable environment.

There are those about who need the vision of my counsel. I have accepted the task without conditions. The souls are already dividing the energy into personalities that will favor the assimilation of the pre-planned lesson.

Whilst perched upon a glimmer of light, my energy awaits the others. It is to be a somewhat difficult maze of experience, which culminates in becoming understanding of conditions. These moments offer the energies the ability to expand beyond the expectations.

It occurs to me that this idea of male/female could only be balanced with great care. Each gender a result of complicated additives that could cause great confusion.

A pinpoint of light approaches, slowly growing larger until it rests next to me, seemingly anticipating my response.

My Soul's Journey Through Some Of My Past Lives
Based Upon True Lives

Session Date: 9-30-15

~2~

Oversoul Perspective Into Mary

As the personalities of the aspects emerged, one stood out amongst them. Withdrawn, lacking in enough self-esteem to conquer the lesson of the feminine, she seemed to fade into the vast tapestry of her surroundings. Her name was Mary, born to parents without the ability to strengthen the weak ego within. Now as an adult, her deep focus upon her plain form and life raise concern for her ability to transcend to evolvement. The other aspects are not without challenges, however, they appear to be coping.

We have decided to intervene to help Mary become more aware of the larger landscape that is available. It is also important for us to support her physically, perhaps as a pet of some degree.

We await her response to our intervention, as the dimensional portal expands.

My Soul's Journey Through Some Of My Past Lives
Based Upon True Lives

Session Date: 8-11-10

~3~

Mary

It was another hot day in the city. Steam rising from the depths of the sewer system accentuating the moisture in the air. A humid heat that left your shirt sticking to your back while you rode the subway to work. Crowded passageways making breathing all but impossible as you wind your way up the stairwell to the heavy sun filled morning that promised more heat by noon day.

I could hardly breathe as I walked the final block to work. Another day of monotony added to the other four that constituted my work week. I stopped marking the days in the calendar long ago. It seemed ridiculous to define my life by the days that seemed so repetitive. All that was really important was that direct deposit every other Friday. An

My Soul's Journey Through Some Of My Past Lives
Based Upon True Lives

endless stream of money that always ended up being inadequate when all was said and done.

For the past year I had taken on another roomie to help defray the non-ending increases of expense in my life. After all, another person in my already crowded apartment seemed irrelevant in the big picture. I really didn't need the privacy that much anyway. My private life was dead-ended in regards to any prospective partners. I was working to live but the extras including boyfriends were elusive.

I suppose I should identify myself if I wish to write my story. A sad one it is for there is really nothing in the immediate present worth noting. I eat. I sleep. I work. There you have the general outline of my life. I wish I were living a more interesting life, one filled with romance and intrigue. Instead I am an overweight lonely girl just trying to make her way.

Way?

My Soul's Journey Through Some Of My Past Lives
Based Upon True Lives

Which way am I going? I am not sure. I only know one thing... my name is Mary. Yes. Mary, a common name for a common girl I guess.

Session Date: 8-12-10

~4~

Mary

My mother used to call me average. I guess she felt relieved that at least I would be able to survive on my own especially if she could marry me off early enough. Unfortunately for her the proposals were not forth coming, causing an increased uncomfortableness the closer to adulthood I approached.

The idea of a job in the big city was enticing to an average girl with no prospects so I escaped as quickly as I could into the abyss of the big city. There my averageness would blend into all of the rest. Perhaps the disappointment would go away as well. So far it had not, but who knew? Maybe there was a shred of hope somewhere.

My Soul's Journey Through Some Of My Past Lives
Based Upon True Lives

Why was my life seemingly so mundane? I don't know. Another drop of sweat slid down my cheek as I approached the office. Hopefully the escape to the air conditioned lobby would erase the stickiness I felt between my shoulders. God! I wish the summer would be over. The heat was almost unbearable. The distance to the door now shorter and within reach. Almost within reach..... Ah! At last relief.

I push the button to the elevator surrounded by anonymous people that I saw every day but did not know. The lack of connection disturbed me but there was too much shyness to bridge the gap to connect with any of them.

There was the good looking fellow who always looked through me followed by the executive sleek woman that always looked like she stepped out of Vogue. I saw these same faces everyday but lacked the ability to know any of them.

Sighing to myself I pushed the button for the 8th floor. Here we go again. Another day. Another moment but nothing other than a paycheck to mark the value of my life. Was this all there was? Stepping out of the elevator I resigned myself to the fact that this was it.

I would live and die in this life being nothing special. Just another body going through the process in a meaningless life with no future.

Grimm with disappointment I sat down at my computer to check email.

Session Date: 8-17-10

~5~

Mary

"You've Got Mail."

The intention of my Internet service provider was to make me feel special. Announcing my mailbox overload seemed like an exciting event for those who might have had none. Of course I realized that my mailbox was a non-entity, but I like to imagine it was a real person delivering my popularity to me on a silver platter. Somehow it made it all a bit more tolerable.

Hmm... Fifteen messages. Most likely all work related as personal stuff was frowned upon by the company.

Here we go...

The first several were advertisements for office supplies. They were followed by requests from the partners in the firm for various documents to be located and delivered to them. Oh, by the way, I am a secretary/receptionist for a law firm. There were seven partners and a few underlings. All of them old enough to be my father.

I saw one of them watching me recently but I never gave him the opportunity to engage in personal conversation. Besides, I wasn't the trophy type that could make an old man look young again. Not pretty enough for that. Besides, he was probably looking because I had gained a few more pounds and my blouse stretched awkwardly across my chest.

"God! I hate old men who stare. There's nothing to see here!"

My Soul's Journey Through Some Of My Past Lives
Based Upon True Lives

He stopped looking towards me as he walked past my desk. Maybe I was mistaken. After all I wasn't all that great to look at.

I felt a sense of emptiness as I began to sort the documents for the head counselor. His name was Robert. He was a fastidious lawyer with a reputation with the ladies. He had been married a few times only to find himself single again when his roving eye caught up with him in the shape of a divorce proceeding.

I needed to settle all these stray thoughts. Needed to focus upon the work of the day. That's what paid the bills so I need to get down to business.

It was after eleven when I finished the morning drill. A few spare moments to make the tea and then start all over again.

I looked out the window, down onto the city street. All of the people looked as significant as a hill of ants. All of them scurrying to their lives not so different and unique as they might think. "What was the point of all this anyway?"

This pondering of life was not going to get my tea made. I had a slew of emails come in while sorting my files and they should be answered before lunch.

There was one tea bag left in the kitchen. I suppose it would fall upon me to get more before the afternoon commenced.

Much to do. Much to do.

"You've Got Mail."

Here we go again. Another afternoon on the horizon as I watch my tea bag begin to steep in the hot water.

Jasmine tea.

My Soul's Journey Through Some Of My Past Lives
Based Upon True Lives

"How did I ever grow to like it so much?" I could not remember. All I knew was that it comforted me even on the busiest of days. Thankfully, I was able to get the last tea bag. Not to have my Jasmine tea would have really wrecked my day. Illogical I know, but true.

I got back down at my desk and noticed an email that appeared to be out of sync with any business that I had dealt with.

"Oh great!"

A spam notice from some astrological site. Hopefully I could delete it before anyone saw it. I was not supposed to have his type of content in my in box.

"Idiots."

I could not delete it.

"You've Got Mail."

My Soul's Journey Through Some Of My Past Lives
Based Upon True Lives

Yes I know I have mail and it needs to go. I took a sip of tea and in the process dribbled some of it down my blouse.

"Oh great." Just what I needed.

Session Date: 8/19/10

~6~

Mary

I reached into my purse to find a tissue to wipe the tea from my blouse. A stain had already formed just below into the first button. Of course my crème colored blouse would just accentuate such an imprint. Feverishly I attempted to wipe the stain clean. I should have known that it would only make it worse.

"You've Got Mail."

"Yes. Yes. I know." I have mail but the stain only grew darker. I felt like crying. The whole day seemed a huge abyss of stain that I could not wipe clean. The emotions were way too high for this. "Why was I becoming so upset?"

I did not know.

Hot tears fell down my check as I finished with the tissue. My blouse now a shambles with tea everywhere, my desk filled with work I had not finished.

"You've Got Mail."

And "Oh Yes" my inbox now overflowing with messages of which it appeared most had nothing to do with work.

I had to get a grip on myself. A deep intake of breath brought me back to reality. Hopefully no one noticed my debacle with the tea. In fact maybe a trip to the ladies room could remove most of it.

"You've Got Mail."

"Enough already." I wiped the tears and leaned towards the computer screen. "Where were all the emails coming from?" It felt like I was going to be buried in correspondence forever.

I pulled my compact out of my purse and attempted to fix the damage to my ravaged emotional face.

There.

A little powder, a little lip gloss and all felt a bit better. Now to attend to business before someone noticed my lack of attention.

As I leaned over to put my purse on the floor, I glanced at the screen again.

All of the emails, perhaps the last four or five, were all from the same address. "www.Past life.?"

"Past life??!!"

"How on Earth did that happen?"

My Soul's Journey Through Some Of My Past Lives
Based Upon True Lives

Nervously I looked around the office. Most were engaged in either telephone conversations or emails. "Thank God!"

If anyone saw this stuff there would be trouble.

"How did this type of stuff get into my email?"

It could be bad news if Robert saw it.

I grabbed my mouse hoping to delete the messages quickly. "Why on Earth was it not happening?"

"Click."

"Click."

"Click, click."

All of them should be erased but some refused to budge. "www.Past life dot what? Oh my God! This could not be worse?"

No matter how I tried.... I even restarted the computer.... I could not get rid of www.Past life dot "trouble". The agitation filled me to the brink of insanity.

I must have looked foolish to anyone passing by. I'm sure if I had been discovered I would have been fired. Beads of sweat not associated with the heat in my air conditioned office lined my upper lip in a procession of embarrassment not known to me before.

"www.Past Life dot something."

In a manic state I finally clicked on the link hoping to find someone in charge to complain to or sue.

"www.Past life dot....whatever."

HASOR

My Soul's Journey Through Some Of My Past Lives
Based Upon True Lives

A ridiculous viewpoint obviously sent by an insane company hoping to bilk me out of money, or more accurately my job.

With resolve I opened the email. I was prepared for idiocy. I was prepared to be hoodwinked, but what I was not prepared for was...

"Hello Mary. We are Hasor."

My Soul's Journey Through Some Of My Past Lives
Based Upon True Lives

Session Date: 9-30-15

~7~

Oversoul

Intro To Sister Francis and Ann

Extending our energy we observed Mary using technology unfamiliar to our understanding. Placing ourselves close to her, we saw the writing of "We are Hasor". Knowing it was not of our doing, we searched through the aspects, finding that it was created from a dream state of our namesake, Hasor.

Surprised, we followed the energy to see the lovely Hasor dreaming of connecting with Mary, but certainly not by expected means. This indicated that the aspects had the ability to bleed through dimensionally. An interesting concept to observe. We await further development and most likely more surprises.

My Soul's Journey Through Some Of My Past Lives
Based Upon True Lives

We sensed a calling from the Ann aspect seeking awareness. We move smoothly through the energy to find her being dropped off at what appears to be a convent.

She is afraid.

9-22-10

~8~

Sr. Francine Xavier

The crisp morning air hit Sr. Francis Xavier in the face as she walked the cloister grounds. A small snowflake fluttered down from the sky landing up her cheek. She raised a rag wrapped hand to wipe the moisture away fearing it would freeze there permanently.

A dark shroud of clouds hovered on the horizon promising more foul weather. Even though it wasn't far, the distance to the church seemed forever away. Once when she first arrived at the convent she counted how many steps it was between each building.

At the time it was a fun distraction from the daily routine imposed upon a novice such as she. Now the number slipped her mind as quickly as she could step on the icy pathway. One foot in front of the other.... she was almost there.

The snow crunched under her feet. It had been a wintry day when she arrived here so long ago. Her name had been just Francine then. A slip of a girl that came to the good sisters to be a servant to God, at least that is what her Papa had said when he left her on the stoop of the sister's home.

The heart of her soul longed to do as he had bid her to do. However, it was hard because the truth was that he could no longer feed her.

To escape disgrace he had offered her to God. She accepted her fate piously although her heart still raced at the thought of her friend Andrew. They had stolen a kiss once behind the livery. It was etched in her mind forever but the truth was she would never see him again.

"What a world where love could not blossom in the hearts of the young."

Daring not to tell Papa, Francine became a novice, consecrating herself to God.

Looking out toward the gate, she saw a glimpse of the newest arrival. There had been no advance notice so it was likely a similar situation to her own. Left at the doorstep as another unwanted daughter, Francine could feel the pain from this distance.

A bewildered young girl turned to bid farewell to a father who had never really seen her. At least not her true self.

Sr. Francine felt a twinge of compassion that led her to the young girl.

"I know her heart. I will assist in any way I can." With that, she entered the chapel to pray for her soul. A vow of silence standing between them like a brick wall.

*My Soul's Journey Through Some Of My Past Lives
Based Upon True Lives*

"I will be with her in spirit, throughout the ordeal.
I have great empathy."

Pulling her rosary out, she began to pray, and
would continue to do so from the stark wooden pew.
She remembered the girl from somewhere. She
would not abandon her.

My Soul's Journey Through Some Of My Past Lives
Based Upon True Lives

Session Date: 2-11-14

~9~

Sister Ann

The early chimes from the chapel awakened Sister Ann well before sunrise. It was her duty to rekindle the kitchen fire before the others came to prepare the morning meal.

Her feet could feel the chill from the stone floor as she relit the dwindling flame. A trip to the well was the next task, so she pulled her veil around her neck as she lifted the heavy iron pot. A cold breath of air greeted her, causing the lungs within her to grimace and moan at the cold air.

Sister Ann hoped the well would not be frozen. Many times she had to chisel an icicle or two with the deep well being frozen over with no ability to retrieve water. Hopefully this morning would render enough water so the outside procession could be minimal.

She knew she must hurry, for the next chime would begin the early prayers of the other sisters. Her participation was expected, so she hurried to find the well abundant with water.

"Praise God!" she exclaimed as she lowered the bucket.

My Soul's Journey Through Some Of My Past Lives
Based Upon True Lives

Session Date: 2-13-14

~10~

Sister Ann

The chapel bells began to chime again, this time beckoning the other nuns to the first devotions of the day. A rustling of their coarse habits blended with the tap of their shoes as they hit the stone floor.

Sister Ann felt lucky to have shoes. Remembering unfortunate earlier circumstances always humbled her into appreciation of the current surroundings. There was shelter, food, and the presence of God. For this a grateful sigh passed her lips as she pulled the huge oak door of the chapel open. It creaked with age, and left Sister Anne wondering how many had walked through its doors.

There were forty-one women and girls in this particular convent. All of them here from early life.

HASOR

My Soul's Journey Through Some Of My Past Lives
Based Upon True Lives

Sister Ann blessed herself with holy water while sliding into a pew already crowded with others who had arrived earlier.

No one glanced up as she knelt. Most were already in deep prayer, awaiting the leadership of the Mother Superior.

The chimes began again, as a slightly bent nun made her way to the lectern.

Session Date: 2-20-14

~11~

Sister Ann

The elderly nun bent from a life of hard work to her bible from the lectern, holding it up for all to see.

"Here is the word of God!" she whispered.

"His goodness and mercy revealed to all who would sin against his good name. Matters of the flesh elevated to our creator are transformed into his higher perspective. Turn away from the body to embrace his love."

Sister Ann felt the shifting of the younger postulates as they listen to Mother Agnes. Some had recently entered the convent so were not entirely devoid of earthly challenges of the body. Having her speak so freely of these things often made postulates uncomfortable at first.

She closed her eyes mouthing the words of the rosary, hoping Mother Agnes would quickly move through her sermon of evil body desires. It was not easy to deny natural physical moments at any age. Even now, her mind would wander to that early day when Geoffrey kissed her behind her humble home. At the time, here heart had fluttered with great hope that he would kiss her again. Alas, he never had the chance. Papa had made his announcement of her sisterhood betrothal to the family at the evening meal.

"God has spoken to me Ann, foretelling your arrival at the Cloister priory. We leave Sunday morrow to deliver you unto your vocation."

With that he began to cut the venison roast that had been prepared for the family. No one stopped to look at her reaction, for it was accepted that Papa's word was final.

She found herself tongue tied and shocked that her destiny would be so clear and final... at least it was to him.

Looking to Mamma for support, she found none. Her eyes remained focused upon her trencher throughout the meal. No one seemed to understand that the idea of Geoffrey's arms around her had been a precursor to her own imagined future. At the age of thirteen, it was time to begin preparations for an adult life. She simply did not dream for a moment that it would be spent in a convent.

Ann was packed and ready after mass. No. There had been no discussion, just Papa sitting in the wagon, brushing the flies away from his eyes. He didn't even acknowledge her tiny form as it climbed into the seat beside him.

No one came to say farewell. The chores of the farm busied everyone from sun up to sun down.

My Soul's Journey Through Some Of My Past Lives
Based Upon True Lives

Ann whispered a goodbye as the horses began to move.   She hoped someone would tell Geoffrey what had happened. Perhaps he would have a hint of her lips as he kissed them.

Session Date: 2-26-14

~12~

Sister Ann

The first days in the convent were difficult. Being alone among all the nuns was confusing. So many rigid rules that seemed to be endless.

Ann's belongings were no longer hers, since now they belonged to everyone. She was asked to change her clothes into a garment of rough fabric which itched and irritated her skin. The linen under garments did little to protect her from its harshness.

Her long braids were spared for the time being. A postulant's head was to remain bare until she took the veil. That was somewhere down the road, so she was told. Time to adjust to the communal group was necessary as the commitment once made, was considered eternal.

My Soul's Journey Through Some Of My Past Lives
Based Upon True Lives

As Ann's father drove away in the wagon, there was a feeling of great loneliness that descended upon her. There was no way of knowing if she would ever see her family again.

Her cell was sparse, having only a small bed and a table. There was a candle upon it that sister Margaret told her was only for brief moments to begin the day. It was not for frivolous use. There was not a window or really any walls. There was a coarse curtain suspended upon a rope to mark off her personal space. The large room was portioned this way to accommodate at least fifteen other postulates.

The first night was filled with the coughs and sputterings of others. Not used to so many in one space, it fell upon her like a roar of noise. Ann did not sleep well, feeling cold as well as lonely.

Was this how it was to be?

Session Date: 2-27-14

~13~

Sister Ann

The night dragged on with Ann staring at the ceiling trying to stay warm. The thin blanket was hardly enough protection from the cold stone floors and walls. She missed sleeping with her sisters back home. Nary a night passed without all of them huddled together for warmth. Here, there was no one.

The chimes from the chapel rang before sun up. A small tap at the door followed by a veiled woman who had been introduced to her as Sr. Francis Xavier poking her head through the curtains.

She signaled it was time to rise with her hands. Why did she not just say so?

*My Soul's Journey Through Some Of My Past Lives
Based Upon True Lives*

Sister Francis turned back towards her with a smile. Taking a step forward, she hugged Ann tightly. The embrace was warm and comforting. Suddenly she felt much better.

With that, the old nun disappeared, as Ann jumped up stunned by how cold the floor was. There was rustling throughout the hall as other postulants awakened to attend mass.

Ann pulled her dress over her head and fastened her shoes to her bare feet.

Session Date: 3-4-14

~14~

Sister Ann

Ann's breath danced in front of her eyes as a fine crystal mist. Keeping her eyes focused to the ground as she gathered sticks, she imagined the mist into a portrayal of a boy and a girl. Each breath manifesting into a dance between them.

Stopping occasionally to adjust here basket, the world she existed in faded away into the embrace of the crystal boy and girl. She imagined that they were destined to be married and to live happily ever after. It was a fable of her own thoughts, never actualized for her in this life.

Her circumstance had led her to the convent and here she must stay. There was no ability to flee.

My Soul's Journey Through Some Of My Past Lives
Based Upon True Lives

Where would she go? Her father had done what was necessary. So be it.

The crystal mist dancers, however, continued to dance all the way through her wood gathering quest. So entranced she was that she did not see the other nuns staring at her from the threshold. Solemn and quiet, they had witnessed her private dance in the garden. Feeling clumsy and exposed, she put the heavily packed basket over her head. A quick return to the doorway allowed her to regain her composure.

"Good morning sisters!" she said, as stoically as she could.

Perhaps they would not guess her secret. None of them knew her other than who she was in the now, the prospective postulant.

As she brushed past them, the obvious judgment was there. Perhaps if she ignored their stares, she would be able to skip any explanation. Bending over her load of wood, she began to kindle the fire.

A few billows of smoke met her face, causing her to cough. She was able to view them as she covered her mouth. None of them had lingered over her, having already moved on to their own chores. Hopefully, they would put aside what they saw, giving it no further thought.

The bells began to ring again as the others moved towards the chapel. Wiping their hands upon their aprons, they moved silently to their places in the pews.

The seat of the wooden bench creaked as Ann sat upon it. Sr. Francis Xavier leaned forward frowning down the row at who was making the noise. Ann froze, hoping she would not be caught. The image of the dances lingered in her head until the Epistle.

She would make the appropriate responses, while dreaming of other things.

My Soul's Journey Through Some Of My Past Lives
Based Upon True Lives

Session Date: 11-24-10

~15~

Clare

If there were three wishes from a magic lamp it would be no contest to what they would be.

I've always felt so alone that the idea of a soulmate has always been intriguing. So that would be my first wish... to meet my soulmate.

The second wish would consist of looking the way I've always imagined myself. It's rather disappointing to see one me in my mind's eye and then encounter the real one in the mirror.

I know it all sounds vain and self-absorbed, but when you've never known perfection the fantasy is needed.

My Soul's Journey Through Some Of My Past Lives
Based Upon True Lives

For the third wish it would again fall under the selfish category, but here it goes.

I would wish for feet that were a size 5. Dainty feminine feet that would complement my beautiful legs.

"Ridiculous? Probably."

"Vain? Absolutely."

It's difficult feeling something other than you are. Sometimes I could swear that I looked entirely different than I do. Of course, most find that observation rather self-serving but it is true. When I look at myself it's always with surprise.

"Why do I feel this way?"

I really don't know. When I was a kid everyone thought I had a vivid imagination, now they just think I'm delusional.

It should make me sad but I cling to this memory like a photo in a gilded e-frame. What I see now is not who I am.

"How could that be true?"

I decide to run above all fear and claim my three wishes. No one will be the master of me. By being in control I have the ability to participate on my terms. Delusional or not, I am in charge, especially with men.

Session Date: 11-17-14

~16~

Clare

It was the best set up I could have imagined. An attractive guy, obviously well off. He purchased an expensive glass of wine, showing he had class as well. Normally I would have ventured into more intimate territory immediately. Normally I didn't care about anything except the objective. A hook-up with an attractive guy to meet my needs and expectations. Everything was perfect. Everything was in motion. However, everything was equally disturbing.

Who was this guy?

I felt like I knew him, but of course I did not. It was not my pattern to even ask a name.

HASOR

My Soul's Journey Through Some Of My Past Lives
Based Upon True Lives

His eyes darted around the room most likely assessing all the women there. Lucky me! He had focused upon me! I should have been pleased. All was going as planned. It was just a matter of time until we finished our drinks. The next move would be to my hotel room. It was my pattern. It was what I did. So why did his scent and smile stop me dead in my tracks?

My Soul's Journey Through Some Of My Past Lives
Based Upon True Lives

Session Date: 9-07-10

~17~

Clare

The sun filled the room with glorious light as Clare pulled the covers up over her head. Stuffed beneath the Egyptian cotton sheets she reached her hand toward the nightstand. A glass toppled to the floor spilling its contents onto the white carpet.

"Crap," she muttered realizing how stale the air was under the sheets. Her inquisitive hand felt the liquid from last night's Pinot dripping to the floor. Imagining the result of the red wine she continued searching for the remote for the curtains.

Successfully she managed to find the television controls before it followed the liquid to the floor. However, it wasn't the television she wished to control. It was the damn sunlight that she could not face at the moment.

More clutter fell before she poked her face out into the light. Eyes squinting, she finally retrieved the small unit and pushed the button.

"Ah, at last."

Her eyes adapted allowing her to survey her bedroom. It wasn't as bad as she imagined. Clothes were tossed precariously about. A souvenir from the local bar clung to the door knob, a silly reminder of yet another conquest.

Lying back against the pillows she ran her hand across the 600 count sheets feeling their softness. Its path halted by the feeling of bare flesh against her fingertips.

A body.

My Soul's Journey Through Some Of My Past Lives
Based Upon True Lives

Clare pulled up the sheet revealing the curly black head of hair that rested there. She closed her eyes trying to remember his name.

"What's in a name anyway?" she asked herself.

"This was just another pilgrim on the road to happiness, wasn't he?"

They had had a good time. That much she remembered, but his name? No.

She slid out of bed and into the shower. The hot beads of water made her focus much sharper, but still she could not recall his name.

It used to embarrass her. Now it was just a game she played until she dried herself off. With any luck she could be dressed and off to work before he awoke. That would only leave the messy detail of writing a polite note and dismissal.

"Was she heartless?"

Yes.

"Was she concerned about the behavior?"

Only in the ability of escaping the inevitable meaningless morning conversation with a handsome stranger. "Or were they beyond that now?"

Clare was not sure why she behaved so. She only knew it was imperative to escape without the drama. Whatever his name was really did not matter. She hated herself for behaving this way, but "Oh Well."

Grabbing her purse she left the note on top of the blanket. He was still snoring loudly guaranteeing an easy departure.

The door clicked behind her as she made her way to the street.

"Was there something wrong with her?"

My Soul's Journey Through Some Of My Past Lives
Based Upon True Lives

She had just left a strange man in her hotel room. Hopefully he would be gone before she got back. There was nothing of value left behind besides her virtue and that was debatable in regards to worth.

Clare shook her head and went on with her day. She would ponder her behavior again later.

~18~

Oversoul

The aspect known as Clare has taken the stance of dominance over the male gender in the only way she feels possible. By being the aggressor in a patriarchal culture, her energy fills a balance in regard to the standard definition of male sexual dominance.

The pattern became one of prominence during childhood, when interaction with male siblings and acquaintances left her feeling weak and overwhelmed.

Wishing to balance that perspective she began to be the aggressor in any sort of physical interaction, thus relieving the feeling of helplessness often felt in other experiences.

We observed the emergence early on in puberty. Hoping to keep a balance in place, we attempted to soothe the lacks of power in other experiences as much as possible.

After careful observation, we intervened by allowing her dream state to become more proactive. By connecting with the other lives there was hope that the bigger picture would reveal to Clare that she was reacting to the influence of other life energy. By blending the experiences slightly, we hoped for a better understanding for the aspect Clare.

We remain steadfast in our concern that she may be becoming unbalanced in the current dramatics as Clare.

The portal to other experience will remain open to help facilitate a broader perspective of who she really is.

Session Date: 9-10-10

~19~

Clare

Conferences always held promise especially if there was travel involved. Each venue offering a variety of experience that was not available in Clare's home town of Milwaukee.

She was a city girl inside. Chicago, New York, and Los Angeles offered so much in the way of culture that she often considered relocating to one of them. In the meantime her conferences would have to fill the void inside her.

She could not just uproot herself to move to a place where she would have no security. Milwaukee was the home office of her job and she would not leave it for the rush of energy in another place where there was not a job opportunity.

My Soul's Journey Through Some Of My Past Lives
Based Upon True Lives

Clare knew that her conflict was deep seeded, perhaps from childhood. The idea of holding onto security was important to her. She felt most happy when her needs were met. The job itself was not the need, security was.

So here she was in Chicago at a conference. Her hook-up from the night before most likely still slumbered in her bed. High heels clicked against the pavement. Feet starting to tingle in her overly expensive shoes. You would think that at the price she paid for them that they would feel like slippers.

Her toes felt crunched while her bunion throbbed in harmony with her heart. If she could walk faster she could most likely get to the meeting on time. The trick was to ignore the pain and push forward.

"Why had she not worn her sneakers?"

They were right there in her suitcase.

"Why?"

Well, because had she rummaged around while still in the room she would have awakened Prince Charming and the awkwardness would have commenced.

What Clare would do for a roll in the hay! She giggled to herself as she walked through the thick glass doors.

Session Date: 9-21-10

~20~

Clare

The sounds of the hotel lobby met Clare as she returned after a long day of meetings. Her feet throbbed longing for a moment of comfort that only a massage could bring. Tomorrow she would wear more comfortable shoes no matter what.

A burst of wind caught her as she opened the ornate outer doors. The outdoor warmth mingled with the air conditioning producing an arid sensation on her cheeks. She closed her eyes and for a moment felt transported to another space. It did not happen often but when it did Clare could almost identify where she was.

My Soul's Journey Through Some Of My Past Lives
Based Upon True Lives

Stepping into the lobby she felt refreshed by the coolness. Now if she could only get upstairs to her room she could take off her shoes and relax.

The hotel was full of people making the lobby feel very crowded. Clare pushed the elevator button waiting somewhat impatiently for its arrival.

The doors of the elevator opened. A group of men moved en mass, causing her to step back to allow them to get through. Sighing to herself as the weight of her briefcase grew heavier, she managed to step between and enter the elevator.

The smell of stale cigars seemed to create a haze above the heads of those who stood in front of her. Obviously smoking was not allowed in the building let alone the elevator. However hazy it was, Clare half closed her eyes trying to stay focused until she got to her room.

"Why was it taking so long?"

It seemed to stop at each floor with a steady stream of embarking and disembarking.

"What floor was it again?"

It was fourteenth floor, only three more to go.

11, 12, 13...

At last the doors opened. Clare pushed forward thankful to be at long last close to her room.

It then dawned on her that when she left it, her rendezvous from the night before was still there.

Certainly by now he would have left, she hoped.

The idea of a second chance was not very appealing. Most men knew the rules of her game for they were usually very similar to theirs.

Meet. Connect. Abandon.

It was a convenient equation she seldom had to convince men of. It was all very tidy and neat.

One more door and she could rest. One more. Now the key. There we are.

The door opened with the hall lit only by the outdoor lights through her room's window. It cast a hazy shadow from the nighttime skylight.

Clare dropped everything in the doorway to remove her now not so great expensive shoes. Making a mental note to never wear them again she reached for the wall switch for the lights.

"I couldn't leave without seeing you one more time," said a thick voice from the other side of the room.

Clare jumped back in surprise as Prince Charming stood up holding a dozen roses in is hand.

Her heart leaped out of her chest as she attempted to step back out of the small hallway, stumbling over her expensive shoes.

Cursing to herself she tried to be calm but ended up releasing a panicked yelp that of course no one would hear through the thick hotel walls and door.

It was very familiar this feeling of being trapped.

"Was she about to be raped or killed?"

She did not know.

The room spun as she tried to remain on her feet.

Her head turned and she found herself in a different room with a thick smell of, Jasmine?

"What was happening?"

My Soul's Journey Through Some Of My Past Lives
Based Upon True Lives

Session Date: 10-27-14

~21~

Clare

Straining her eyes in the firelight, she tried to see "Prince Charming" closer. What on earth was happening?

The hotel room glistened with an unfamiliar radiance she had not noticed before. The furniture was different, while the thick carpet?, Rug?, Or whatever this was, felt soft beneath her. The man coming towards her resembled Prince Charming a little, but as he got closer it clearly was someone else.

He stood facing her as if he was inspecting her. A tremor of fear gripped her tightly. Was he going to harm her, or what?

My Soul's Journey Through Some Of My Past Lives
Based Upon True Lives

Obviously she had been transported to another location. Did he drug her? Knock her out? What? What? What?

To her surprise, Clare felt the warmth of an open fire. There were lengths of transparent colored cloths hanging in all directions of this place.

Good god! Was this heaven!

There was a fragrance of Jasmine mixed with the heavy scent of musk as the man moved towards her. He was attired in a long tunic. His hair appeared long and greasy, but groomed.

Session Date: 11-05-14

~22~

Clare

The clock said 7:21, obviously it was morning. The sun glared through the crack in the curtains. Not wanting to face the day yet, I fell upon the bed hoping for additional zzz's.

My mind raced through the events that I remembered from last night. Every detail was vivid. I examined myself for any telltale signs, but there were none. I felt like I had been awake all night being with a man I thought had abducted me.

Apparently that was not the case.

I did not have any appointments this day as I had planned on what I called a "scouting day".

My Soul's Journey Through Some Of My Past Lives
Based Upon True Lives

Business was finished, so, I had planned an extra day of R&R. Normally I would find an expensive bar/restaurant while decked out in my fanciest attire. Never knew what I would encounter, and that was half the fun.

My Soul's Journey Through Some Of My Past Lives
Based Upon True Lives

Session Date: 11-6-14

~23~

Clare

As I looked around my hotel room, all the formal plans were suspended. Whatever had happened, it left me wobbly in my stance.

Was it a dream?

I didn't know where the dream left off and reality began. The man kept calling me Hasor? I couldn't begin to spell it, let alone figure out why that was such a big deal, but it was.

After splashing my face with water, I took off yesterday's clothing. Rumpled! That's how I felt, rumpled! I slipped into my robe, deciding to take the day slowly.

Never had I had such a vivid dream before. The fragrance followed me here to this room. Couldn't place it, but it was nice.

I should have stopped allowing an obvious dream to keep interrupting my thoughts. Maybe if I got showered and dressed I would feel better.

The day was still young. There was a beautiful sun shining, and a fresh day to be lived.

The hot water/steam did its best to invigorate my mood. However, the vivid images of the night before continued to haunt my every move. Determined as I was to enjoy my "free" day, there remained a whisper in my thoughts that I simply could not dismiss as a dream.

Session Date: 11-8-14

~24~

Clare

The day passed swiftly while I enjoyed some shopping. The big city provided many choices that robbed my bank account. I chose to purchase a silk black dress, with a pair of black pumps. Of course I had a lot of slinky black dresses, but convinced myself I need to have yet another. Tonight I would be out looking for romance of the best kind. Just wanted to regain my footing by looking fabulous.

Cocktail hour was upon me before I thought of last night's debacle again. The dream was so real, but obviously I was just plain exhausted, and merely fell asleep. No excitement this night. All would go as usual this evening. With luck, there would be connection. I spritzed my hair to hold it in place, while gathering my purse articles for a spectacular night.

Tonight would not be spent dreaming. It would all be real, of that I was sure.

The evening unfolded the way I expected. Sitting at the bar the energy felt electrifying. Music waved softly over me as I closed my eyes. Lost in own fantasy, I felt someone sit down next to me. Immediately I remembered the scent from somewhere. My eyes flew open, expecting one scene, but another was already in progress.

He was attractive. His smile lit up half the room, however, it was the cologne that peaked my interest. Turning towards him to get a better look, I found myself practically nose to nose with him.

Who was he?

I vaguely felt a strange familiarity.

*My Soul's Journey Through Some Of My Past Lives
Based Upon True Lives*

Session Date: 11-23-14

~25~

Oversoul

The focus of the Oversoul is constantly in motion. Each assigned aspect/personality requires support beyond what they experience in their realities. We embrace the energy with love and understanding, while adding our own burst of power whenever possible.

It is important to grasp the concept of multiple incarnations so that a realization of the true process can be absorbed and comprehended.

Each soul has an awareness of the other outside of the process. It is only while engaged in a life does the realization of the interconnection become blurred.

HASOR

*My Soul's Journey Through Some Of My Past Lives
Based Upon True Lives*

We share this perspective in the story of Hasor.

My Soul's Journey Through Some Of My Past Lives
Based Upon True Lives

Session Date: 9-27-10

~26~

HASOR

Before the 1st Life

The energy sprang forward in full anticipation of the opportunity. Feelings emerged as the idea of the coming experience began to take form.

Being conscious for the first time, a moment of what it would be like started as a thought. A small one yes, but a vision of being solid transforming the energy until the union.

The core of the whole allowed this small fragment to take hold in the small seed of life. The evolvement of this now physical body became larger until the entrance was inevitable.

It was female. Perhaps not the first choice of an alpha male, the birth father, but at least the fruitfulness of the delivery would repeat itself until the full measure of sons could be procured.

During this time special care was given to the mother indulging her every whim. For her body was no longer hers alone. Now it was an instrument of the gods!

The waiting began at first light. Frightful it was to be plunged into the darkness, not knowing what awaited. Such as it was for this energy... the time of waiting an opportunity to explore the feeling of this body, this vessel.

The energy was aware early on of its destiny. Words of this experience had been heard, and they were correct. It was a moment of expression like no other.

Physical being was a golden moment not easily done. Ah, there had been stories of failure, however, this one would be successful. The female energy saw to it. Cerebral as it was, the most fascinating part of this agreement was this sense of touch. An energy exchange like no other.

She slid easily through the passage into the hands of a stern midwife who took this moment very seriously. Dust moved outside the delivery in great clouds of confusion. The sweat dripped from the brow of the mother.

"Success!"

The child lived. Immediately the midwife washed the child cleansing the small face so that it could breathe on its own.

"What shall you call your new daughter?" the mother was asked.

The air was thick with heat as the family leaned in to hear the faint whisper of the exhausted mother.

"Hasor," she said with her eyes closed. "Hasor".

With that she fell into a deep slumber, a cool cloth upon her forehead to soothe her.

The girl child opened its eyes with a deep cry from its perfect lips. The journey ending here was a surprise so quick had the entry been.

Little fingers began to smooth themselves across the face of the mother. Hasor had arrived safely. The senses kicking in for her first introduction to the physical.

Hasor

I feel the smoothness of my form. The sounds are as they were described. I could feel the vibration and it was beautiful.

My Soul's Journey Through Some Of My Past Lives
Based Upon True Lives

Session Date: 9-28-10

~27~

Hasor

First Incarnation

Intellectually I was able to somewhat prepare for the experience. As my thoughts created each movement I became fascinated first with the sense of touch. Incredible ripples of energy greeted my fingertips almost at once. The sight was dim and not available. Disappointing, but certainly I had been made aware of the development necessary.

Vibration hit the small piece of membrane resonating tonally in a way I was not quite prepared for. I found that the higher the frequency the more able I was to "hear" it. It was much more interesting than I imagined before coming to this place of being.

My Soul's Journey Through Some Of My Past Lives
Based Upon True Lives

A fragrance of something hit my nose before I was quite prepared. It affected me emotionally and I felt myself with a surge of what was called emotion. I cried with the water of eyes until my mother soothed me with the touch of her finger tips... this whole idea of sensing more provocative than I thought.

Almost immediately was a feeling of emptiness. I did not understand the sensation so I responded with a wail of my own.

"What was wrong? Did the process become unavailable?"

I could not search properly for the answer so I continue my own wail of vibration.

Surprisingly I was met by the bosom of the mother. Her form pressed against my open mouth inserting her skin until my mouth received a fluid. It stilled the emptiness allowing me to connect in a way not known.

HASOR

My Soul's Journey Through Some Of My Past Lives
Based Upon True Lives

I began to feel full of energy while the fears that had arisen subsided. I could feel the goodness and love of the mother. I looked deep into her face noticing her eyes as they beheld me. We connected deeply and I relaxed into the nurture of her caress. This would be a better experience now, as I had hoped.

My Soul's Journey Through Some Of My Past Lives
Based Upon True Lives

Session Date: 9-29-10

~28~

Hasor

(First Incarnation)

The sensations aroused in me a passion. All of my physical senses engaged themselves, leaving me in a whirlwind of energy. This was much more than described. The idea of the "I" settling within until I had identity. Being a part of the whole, then being a whole person was intriguing.

I could feel the energy from those who were deemed as family. There was recognition of familiars who had taken form before me. This was a true experience as I was embraced by those who had known me, and those who wished to.

HASOR

My Soul's Journey Through Some Of My Past Lives
Based Upon True Lives

The exact time was foreign to me but there was sensing of the passage. Again that was new since this was the first engagement.

Being female suited me. My mother was nurturing. Her hands fluttered about in an effort to soothe and comfort me.

There was, however, a feeling of disappointment from he who was the father. I still did not have full appreciation of the significance of gender. My only experience was that of female, which suited how I felt. Perhaps the father would reverse the opinion after he had a chance to know me.

The ways of physical still fresh would take time (another thing that lacked understanding). I had been advised of these things. My only hope was that I would remember.

My form developed while I pondered all that I have spoken of. Time passed interestingly enough. All thought of me rather useless and undeveloped. I,

My Soul's Journey Through Some Of My Past Lives
Based Upon True Lives

on the other hand, anticipated a moment where I could render my true essence and be truly a human being.

"Was that not the goal?"

My Soul's Journey Through Some Of My Past Lives
Based Upon True Lives

Session Date: 2-6-14

~29~

HASOR

<u>Oversoul</u>

Balancing a pinpoint of light energy into the void is not always an easy task. The twinkle of electrons swirling creates an effervescent image that the energy glides upon in its search for experience. Such was the moment the Oversoul created in this focal point in reality.

There were many such energies that had evolved to this stage of participation. Suddenly not so focused upon their own experience, they moved to a precipice of greater vision. It was time to create a new dimension of evolution, having finished the individual evolvement.

My Soul's Journey Through Some Of My Past Lives
Based Upon True Lives

So it was for the small flicker of light as it looked upon physical reality. There were several opportunities that peeled back the Oversoul as it found its place of perspective.

A single train of thought emanated from the light. An assignment of other souls, who would need guidance paraded their plans before the higher realms. A moment of reflection as the first soul moved towards its incarnation.

What would it create?

What would it experience?

How would the Oversoul maintain the connection when the soul moves through the life with free will in place?

No answers were forth coming. The Oversoul positioned itself to view the birth. As the energy took over the physical form, the Oversoul smiled with great enthusiasm. It was to be a female, perhaps the first endeavor into that perspective.

A huge wail of surprise from the small soul as it exercised its new lungs. Red faced and anxious, the baby continued to wail endlessly. Perhaps the birth was too intense? Perhaps the body was malfunctioning in some way?

The Oversoul leaned forward from the point of light to send soothing tones to quiet the baby.

"Rest my little one, all will be well".

The babe was swaddled in linen and took to her mother's breast quickly. The silence of the connection between mother and child complete.

The Oversoul felt pleased as it observed the warm moment.

"Ah, it is well that she feels the sense of belonging. There is great opportunity to learn the perspective of female in that form."

Energetic fingers brushed the brow of the baby. The mother kissed the little head, which already sported a lush dark hairline.

The Oversoul felt blessed that it had all gone so well. A warm sensation filled the Oversoul's heart as it observed.

The physical mother whispered to the child "Welcome my child. Welcome to this world. I will name you Hasor, a proud name for a strong woman."

Hasor?

The Oversoul was touched, while extending herself to both mother and child.

"What an honor," whispered the Oversoul.

"She is named after me."

With that, the Oversoul HASOR turned her attention away, allowing the mother and child to bond.

My Soul's Journey Through Some Of My Past Lives
Based Upon True Lives

Session Date: 8-20-10

~30~

Hasor

The mist lingered over the river like a cloudy day. Normally the air was cooled by its tentacles of moisture. This day was not to be so. Already the wet air pressed against me in desperation. It seemed the world was changing quickly as I longed for the days of my childhood.

Often the dryness would ruin the crop or the outcome of a day of ritual. No more. I rather enjoyed the way the mist left my skin. I felt invigorated as I studied my face at the river's edge.

Twelve years today I had been born to a family of prosper. Never had the day been so bright and alluring. My bracelets clinked together creating a

My Soul's Journey Through Some Of My Past Lives
Based Upon True Lives

rhythm of sound that made me want to dance in the arms of the sun.

Ah but the sun hid behind the mist waiting for the perfect time of arrival. Until then I would amuse myself with the river and its charms. After all, the Maturing Ceremony making me into a woman would not begin for some time. Perhaps other amusements would find their way.

One must anticipate what one wants, or so my grandmother told me. I often think of her and the ways of women. I wish to know more of the secrets but alas must await their arrival.

Again the tinkling of jewelry reminds me of the time at hand.

My Soul's Journey Through Some Of My Past Lives
Based Upon True Lives

Session Date: 8-24-10

~31~

Hasor

The steps toward adulthood were etched in my mind as vivid as the reeds of the river. A gentle breeze causing a ripple in their stature made for a quiet calming moment for all who witnessed it.

I could hear the faint cry of the heron as it flew towards the river from the vast sea that I had heard about, but never seen. Tales of others not like us filled the feasts given by my Father who had been many places, far more than my mother who demurred to his every wish.

Such was the way with women. Stories only from those who have seen never firsthand experience, but a moment shared by others. It was always a blessing to hear the vivid details of a great story teller while partaking at one of the many meals with my family. Of course the best seats reserved for my brothers and Father who remained the important aspects of my family.

Perhaps if I had been born a male I would not have to listen, but be the speaker of all the adventure.

My Father winked at me across the table as he sipped his wine. I knew he felt blessed by Yahweh especially since he was so fruitful with my mother. They still felt the love since it was evident in their eyes.

There were fourteen of us. My place amongst the daughters honored for I was the oldest. I would be the first to become a woman. The feeling of the sensual aroused within me without the proper preparation. My mother told me of the ways of men but it had not felt real quite yet. Supposedly the steps to womanhood would follow with a marriage treaty. One that would please my Father and honor my family.

I wondered who would be chosen. "Would they stir my loins in the way my mother spoke of?"

My cheeks flushed at the thought and I hoped no one noticed my self imposed embarrassment.

I turned my head back to the mist. It was there I felt comfort with myself and my womanly ways. I still had no idea what they were, but I awaited them with anticipation.

My Soul's Journey Through Some Of My Past Lives
Based Upon True Lives

8-26-10

~**32**~

Hasor

At noon day the mist was etched in sunlight as it diminished into nothingness. The air was heavier due to the heat. It was now when those who were working would stop for a rest.

My abode would be quiet with only the hum of insects to mark it. I lay upon my mat trying to beckon sleep. Of course it would not indulge me so I stared at the curtains wondering how long it would take for the sun to diminish. I despised this imposition upon my day. It was expected for me to retire but my heart wanted to leap with joy.

It had been revealed that my Father was in negotiations for my marriage. The details not known but just the imagined moment was enough to set my heart beating rapidly.

This was the moment sacred to all girls about to become women. The match that would define the rest of my life. I hoped for a man of prosper and beauty but knew that whatever befell me was to be accepted without hesitation.

Giggling to myself I tossed and turned in the midday sun awaiting a cooler evening. I wanted to speak to my mother to get confirmation about the marriage. All the hearsay was most likely not accurate. I had hopes that Mother would have more information so that my dreams could take their place in reality.

I looked out at the garden withering in the heat. It amazed me that so much could change in a mere few hours. My sari draped around me was starting to be moistened by my own perspiration. It was an uncomfortable feeling, as I felt beads of water accumulate at my neckline. I called for a servant to cool me with a damp cloth, but even that did not soothe the heat of the day.

"How long till the darkness would embrace the day?"

It would be only then that relief would come.

I studied my feet as I held them up. They were caked with sand from my early morning walk. Perhaps I should have cleansed them in the water but at the time I was more preoccupied with the mist.

My Soul's Journey Through Some Of My Past Lives
Based Upon True Lives

Session Date: 8-31-10

~**33**~

Hasor

I rolled over onto my stomach propping my chin up with my hands. The small openings in the window casings offered a bright view of the sand as the sun bounced off its many pebbles.

In the distance a cloud of dust began to form. Bellowing high into the sky it could only mean that others were on their way to our compound. It was not often that visitors came upon us. A voice called out of the impending arrival. They were still too far away to be able to distinguish their identities.

I sat up straining to see from my mat who they might be. In younger times the excitement would have been allowed. Now on the verge of womanhood, my aloofness was expected.

My Soul's Journey Through Some Of My Past Lives
Based Upon True Lives

Hovering between the girlhood giddishness and my new found womanly ways I rose up to my knees attempting to compromise my true feelings with those that were now expected of me.

Three men. That is what it looked like from my place of observation. The faces draped in cloth to protect them from the elements left little opportunity to identify them.

Perhaps I should prepare for guests. My father would have summoned for me by now. Or maybe he was unaware of their identity as well.

I pressed my eye against the small opening hoping for more enlightenment.

"Who were they? Why were there no preparations being made?"

It was custom to invite all travelers to the fete for food and drink. I had hoped this was the time of decision. The thought of meeting someone who might become my husband was a fearsome moment for me.

"Would I be liked? Would he love me at first sight?"

All of these questions moved through my mind as I pressed closer to the small opening hoping for confirmation that this indeed would be him.

"Was I just a girl with a fantasy, or would this be the great betrothal?"

I didn't notice when my mother appeared in the doorway, so absorbed in my spying, her presence did not distract me from my quest.

"Hasor."

I bumped my head on the encasement as I abruptly turned around. My head pulled back in pain, I reeled around to face the voice of my mother.

My Soul's Journey Through Some Of My Past Lives
Based Upon True Lives

"Hasor!"

"Yes ma'am."

I managed a respectful bow just in time to see my
mother move towards me with a scowl.

"What are you doing?"

"Nothing Ma'am."

"Nothing?"

"By the gods, if you bring embarrassment to your
father this day I will beat you to death," she snarled.

Oh yes. I forgot to tell you about my mother.
It's usually a subject I refrain from in hopes she will
never materialize too closely to my person.

My mother was harsh as a mother should be for a daughter like me. I had a habit of missing important keys to being the perfect woman. Or so she told me.

Anyway, I was now facing her wrath, attempting to create a sound reason for standing tip toe upon my mat in observation of outside things that I should have no knowledge of.

It was not a great way to start a conversation with my mother. I closed my eyes awaiting the inevitable reprimand.

Behind the mask I wore for my mother was an image of a woman who did not value herself. I despised the feeling of worthlessness my mother instilled in me. I wished to comfort her as I moved deeper into the day dream. The pounding tone of my mother's voice rambled on as I sought the woman. I imagined her name as Mary. Just simply Mary. She was vacant in her emotions. I wished her not hear the attacks of my mother. I soothed the rough edges as I continued down the dream path. If I could catch up with her, I would be happy. Chiseling a message into a tree would be helpful, but what would I say?

Hello Mary? It's me Hasor? What could that possibly mean to her?

"Are you listening to me Hasor?" My mother's grating voice demolishing my dream haven, dumping me back into her presence.

"Of course Mamon, I am listening," I replied respectfully.

My Soul's Journey Through Some Of My Past Lives
Based Upon True Lives

Session Date: 1-22-14

~34~

Mary

Hasor?

Who on earth was Hasor?

I did not know anyone by that name! I moved the mouse across the pad, hoping to retrieve where this instant message was coming from.

The screen went dark momentarily, then flashed a mosaic pattern a few times before presenting a blank screen. I felt confused and a bit scared that my computer may have imploded somehow. My mind raced into all the files and correspondence that would disappear should my computer default.

Click, click, click.

No response.   Just a now white screen that spelled disaster for me here at work.

A colleague heard my laments and came over to help.

"Perhaps we should turn off the computer and restart it?"

His name was Tom.   He was always pleasant to me, but had never ever ventured near my desk during the work day.   His voice startled me in my intense anxiousness.

"I guess so," I replied, rather despondently.

Tom reached under the desk and flipped the switch to off.   My computer sighed while the screen went dark. I could hear the hum of the hard drive as it settled into silence.

"Don't worry," Tom said.

My Soul's Journey Through Some Of My Past Lives
Based Upon True Lives

"Sometimes they just need a few moments to settle down. You shouldn't lose anything except for what you might have been working on. You didn't happen to save it, did you?"

I actually could not even remember if I had been working on something. My mind was racing in all different directions trying to figure out who Hasor was.

"Um, yes. Yes I did," I mumbled as Tom flipped the computer power back on.

"Give it a few minutes. The reboot should do wonders to get everything back on line," said Tom.

I whispered a feeble "Thank you," as Tom nonchalantly walked back to his desk. I could feel beads of sweat forming on my brow. Why was I so nervous? None of it made any sense.

My Soul's Journey Through Some Of My Past Lives
Based Upon True Lives

Session Date: 1-23-14

~35~

Mary

I sat staring at my computer screen as it slowly rebooted itself. All of the files were flashing before me one by one. That in itself was quite a relief. My heart had stopped pounding in my chest as the completion of the programs finished initializing.

Tom had gone back to his work. Apparently he thought the reboot would fix everything. Did he think my hysteria was a bit overdone? Ugh! I spent way too much time thinking about what other people thought or didn't think about me.

At least my computer appeared to have returned to normal. Everything was working, but I wanted to see where the message from this Hasor had come from. Surely there would be a trail that would lead me to where the message had come from.

Surely.

I began to search for the message, however, my efforts were not rewarded. Spending close to a half hour looking, brought me no closer to the answer.

What had happened to it?

Frustrated, I knew I had to return to my work. Management would see my distraction and become disturbed, so I ceased searching. It would have to wait until this evening. I decided to stay after work to solve the mystery.

Hasor.

I sounded like an Egyptian name or something. Certainly not a modern name, perhaps an ancient one.

My Soul's Journey Through Some Of My Past Lives
Based Upon True Lives

The day moved slowly and soon I was mired knee deep in briefs. It all had to be sorted efficiently, thus I abandoned this Hasor. At least for the time being.

My Soul's Journey Through Some Of My Past Lives
Based Upon True Lives

Session Date: 1-26-14

~36~

Mary

By the time the day finished, my head ached from staring at the computer screen.   As much as I wanted to investigate what had occurred earlier in the day, I decided to close down and go home.

The office emptied quickly at 5 PM. Everyone seemed to have somewhere to go. Exit energy was abundant as I gathered my things. Tom was already at the elevator tapping his foot when I turned the corner.

"Did your computer hold up?" he asked while pushing the elevator button.

My Soul's Journey Through Some Of My Past Lives
Based Upon True Lives

Nodding my head while following him into the crowded elevator, I thought I should ask him if websites could just pop up on the screen.

"Well, maybe an advertisement could," he replied.

"I had a weird experience right before it crashed," I replied.

There was something about Past Lives, and then there was something like and instant message that said "hello" to me by name, and then said she/he was Hasor?

Tom laughed out loud.

"Probably an ad, but maybe you searched it earlier? You don't believe in all that crap, do you?"

I felt my face getting hot with embarrassment. Perhaps that was too much information to give Tom. Would he gossip with others about me?

I stopped talking, hoping for it to just all go away. If I were going to get to the bottom of it, certainly there would be no help from Tom.

The elevator descended slowly. Crowded and stuffy, the only sound now was muffled and snarling noises. Hopefully no one had heard any of our exchange.

Finally!

Arrival to the lobby floor brought release from the day. Clamoring to get out, I could feel the breath of people behind me anxious to go home.

Tom winked at me with a smug grin. I could tell he would remember and give me trouble in the days to come. Oh, I shouldn't call it trouble, but extended teasing surely was written in his eyes.

"See you Monday," he whispered as he turned toward the parking garage.

"Yes you will," I responded.

Home would be welcomed. It had been a long day, long week, and yes, long life.

Session Date: 10-07-15

~37~

Oversoul

It is of great interest that Mary and Hasor would be connecting in this way. The power of the soul always providing new perspective.

Realizing that Mary needed extra support, the decision to provide that was asked of the familiar single guides around her.

The image of a comforting being was decided upon and the "cat" was created. A guide took up residence. The rest unfolded nicely, the cat became her companion.

All were surprised she named her Jasmine.

Session Date: 1-27-14

~38~

Mary

In the privacy of my apartment, I slipped off my shoes and sank into the sofa. The world was blocked out and I was often at peace.

Oh yes, and there was also my cat I had christened "Jasmine". She was a tiny thing that had showed up in front of my building a few years ago. At the time bedraggled and hungry, I had watched in horror as she ran across the busy street right into my hands. I had thought for sure she would be road kill.

Normally, scared kitties were afraid of humans. This one started purring as soon as I touched her. Carrying her upstairs, I wrapped her in a blanket, sat her on the couch, all the while rummaging through my cupboards for something to feed her.

By the end of the week, she was a permanent resident. I marveled at how she had integrated herself into my life.

I had always been a loner on all levels, and somehow this ball of fur had staked her claim in my life. To this day, I am not certain how it happened, but it did.

I came up with the name Jasmine from a childhood story I had read as a child. It seemed to fit her, and I think Jasmine was a princess of sorts. Since she spent most of her day upon her pillow throne, it seemed fitting.

Something about her brought me comfort. No matter how the day had gone, being in her presence gave me great happiness.

Laughingly I call her my soulmate kitty. Her purrs began with my key in the door. They never diminished until she was asleep, or I was leaving the next morning.

We were more deeply connected than any other living creature in my world. For this I felt blessed.

Tonight I put her in my lap feeling the soft fur with my fingertips. Jasmine relaxed while I stoked her. I could have sat there all night, and I often did.

Soft flutes were playing on the radio and left me transfixed upon the lights from the street. Gazing out at the city, I felt good. So what if I was alone? I needed to grab onto what I did have. Exactly what that was, I didn't know. Tonight, however, it was Jasmine and me. Somehow that was enough for right now.

My Soul's Journey Through Some Of My Past Lives
Based Upon True Lives

Session Date: 2-1-14

~39~

Mary

The alarm went off earlier than usual. For some reason it was 5:30 AM instead of 6:30 AM. It was irritating because as soon as I open my eyes, I am awake. Jasmine slipped back under the covers, annoyed that I had disturbed her warm spot. Fortunately for her, she returned to slumber quickly.

I, on the other hand, immediately jumped into the shower to begin the day. Lucky pussy cat!

The steam from the shower filled the bathroom, casting an ethereal glow from the florescent lights. Closing my eyes, I could feel the pulse of the water as it cascaded down my back.

HASOR

My Soul's Journey Through Some Of My Past Lives
Based Upon True Lives

I took a bit of extra time, as I was up so early. A bit of pampering was a good way to begin the day. I must have stood there with my eyes closed for 10 minutes or more. Slowly, I encouraged myself to shut off the water and step out into the densely steamed room.

A fluffy towel from the rack felt even better, as I dried myself off. I saw my reflection muted by the steam in the mirror. Funny, how it tricked your mind into seeing other images.

I focused upon my face, but mutely there appeared to be other forms. Wow, I needed to wake up.

The blurred images started to take shape. What they were revealing wasn't truly clear.

I reached forward with my hand to wipe the condensation off the image. All it did was make the image more clear.

I reached forward with my hand to again wipe the condensation off the image. All it did was make the image more clear. There were people milling about in my bathroom!

Stifling a scream, I turned to see it all more clearly. Of course I was met by my towel rack and a painting of shells from the seashore! My mind apparently was playing tricks upon me. I had to wake up.

Wrapping a towel around me, I opened the bathroom door. Jasmine ran in, having some sort of hissy fit. She jumped up on the counter, staring deliberately into the fogged vanity mirror. Her hissing ceased, but she stared intently into the fog. What was she seeing?

I leaned into her, fixing my gaze in alignment with hers. There was something there! People moving about as if they were not aware of me? It was not behind me. It was there, right there, in front of me. Jasmine and I stood transfixed, watching another unfold in front of us. What on Earth was going on?

My Soul's Journey Through Some Of My Past Lives
Based Upon True Lives

Session Date: 2-2-14

~40~

Mary

There was a strange scent that startled me out of my self-imposed trance. I could still see movement in front of me, but I also knew I was still in my bathroom. There were women dressed strangely that seemed to be in deep conversation with each other. They wore harem looking outfits, not from any time period I could identify. I leaned into the mirror hoping to hear what was being discussed, but alas, Jasmine began to meow loudly and the whole vision suddenly folded up in front of me.

I stood there for a moment, feeling very disconnected. Jasmine rubbed up against my hand, demanding an ear rub, so of course I indulged her. Trying to piece together what just occurred was troubling. Was I hallucinating?

Placing my hands on the counter top, I gazed back at my now reflection in the mirror. Yup, I was still in one piece, but what just happened was beyond bizarre.

Session Date: 2-4-14

~41~

Mary

By the time I got myself dressed and out the door, my mind was reeling. I figured I had missed my commuter train, so I opened my garage door to start my little Volvo. If I focused, I might make it to work close to "on time".

Being alone in the car, I reflected upon the events of the past few days. The weird computer event and the foggy mirror were stand outs in a series of odd events. When I arrived at work today, I was going to get to the bottom of the past life drama. It must have been a marketing ploy. One that I simply would not tolerate!

Exploring the website would be one of the first things I did today. Hopefully there was a contact number so I could call and complain about their under handed tactics.

Just thinking about it made my blood boil. They surely had some sort of spyware that confiscated an individual's information. Sending an instant message saying this odd name of "Hasor" was really over the top.

The mirror event of this morning could be explained by the fact I was probably still half asleep. Surely yesterday's computer debacle was causing me to be a bit disconnected from my reality. Yes, of course it was.

My Soul's Journey Through Some Of My Past Lives
Based Upon True Lives

Session Date: 9-03-10

~42~

Hasor

If I tilt my head back far enough I can see all the stars. Many nights I have stayed outside to feel the cool night air. Since an early age the sky has held much fascination for me.

My elder brother Nafir would sit with me so that I would not be alone. Often he would tell me stories about the shapes that the stars would make. I would giggle with delight when he would surprise and scare me when I became too intrigued with the story.

In these intimate times with my brother the smell of Jasmine would fill our noses with aroma. The blossoms at their earliest were the most fragrant. My mother would gather the petals to make the tea to end my day.

Often the taste would transform any difficulty I might be having in my day. Soothing, fragrant, the steam would fill my head and soul with comfort. I never missed a cup nor did I ever miss the blossoms when they first would appear.

Nafir would appreciate the fragrance but always declined the tea. I suppose it was a sign that it had spiritual powers only for me. I liked that. Knowing that something as exquisite as the Jasmine would be only for me.

As I grew to maturity the tea also soothed my womanly ways. My mother approved, surprisingly. It was probably the only thing she ever approved of in regard to me.

The silence of the night sky was upon me again when I realized how much of a woman I was becoming.

My Soul's Journey Through Some Of My Past Lives
Based Upon True Lives

My brother would hold my hand on those occasions offering me the support Mother and Father never did. I loved Nafir for that. I wished always to be in his presence, however, that was not to be. The day came where my marriage was immanent and it was now.

A messenger came through the door with news for my father. Mother came whispering to me to be ready. So it was.

"Who was he to be?"

Beads of perspiration rolled down the center of my back. I tried to look grown up but felt younger than my years. Suddenly seeking my brother's hand I realized I would hold it no more. Girlhood was completed. I was about to be a woman. Ready or not.

My Soul's Journey Through Some Of My Past Lives
Based Upon True Lives

Session Date: 1-17-14

~43~

Hasor

Adorned with the finest, I waited behind the curtain ready to receive the guests of my father. My best peeking through holes of light did not begin to provide the enlightenment I desired. I knew that the three men had dined with my father, their murmurs not decipherable to my ears.

Was one of them my future husband?

It was not clear. The clink of cups signified a deal, or at least it sounded that way. My heart pounded in my chest, while my eyes desired to see who he would be.

My Soul's Journey Through Some Of My Past Lives
Based Upon True Lives

The curtain parted and I could see the four of them seated by the fire. A light smoky haze from their pipes did not allow for clear vision.

A boy with a flute had begun a lingering song that relaxed my soul a little. Of course I would be anxious, my destiny sitting upon one of three cushions just a few feet away.

I paused a moment before stepping into the lit arena, attempting to stop the mild shaking I was experiencing.

In that moment my ambitious mother managed to press her bony fingers in my back, causing me to stumble forward. It was not how I imagined as I struggled to maintain my balance.

Fortunately, my face partially covered allowed for my embarrassment to go undetected.

HASOR

My Soul's Journey Through Some Of My Past Lives
Based Upon True Lives

I felt the carpet become softer as I neared their circle. All eyes upon me, I lowered mine in submission.

Would my husband take my hand?

I did not know. I bowed in reverence to all of them.

Please.

Please be charming.

Not too old to appreciate the freshness of my spirit, I stood there expectantly for what seemed like a lifetime. The flute danced in my ears as my eyes searched the floor for movement towards me.

Session Date: 1-18-14

~44~

Hasor

His shoes were of the finest cloth, stitched with gold. They made no sound as they made their way towards me. There was a musky smell I could not identify.

I raised my hand upwards to accept his hand. He lifted me like a feather to my feet. I caught my breath before the first glance. What if the face that looked back upon me was not pleasing?

No matter, what there was need of, was non-reaction from me, especially if the connection was not a good one.

It mattered not how I felt. My duty to my family came before my feelings. My response was not what mattered. It would be my ability to please my husband with my womanly ways. There had been no preparation for my ways to come forward. My mother had stated that it was my responsibility to be seductive to him. I was not entirely sure what was expected, other than my total submission.

His hands were soft. They felt like silk as they grasped mine. I was lifted to my feet as his eyes met mine. They were brown and seemed to look deep within my soul.

My face still covered, revealed only a shadow of my features. He kissed my hand with soft lips and led me to the table.

"Behold, my bride."

There were acknowledgements from the others. My father appeared pleased, so hopefully my behavior had been sufficient.

My Soul's Journey Through Some Of My Past Lives
Based Upon True Lives

His name was Bak-ran, or so he said. I was not able to stay longer. Whisked away by the women to prepare for the wedding, left me unsure of what had just happened. I was not certain of exactly how he looked, it all happened so quickly.

The four men drank to their good fortune for making such a match. I retreated to the sanctity of my chambers to await the ceremony. His scent lingered upon my hand as my hair was combed for retirement. It felt better to have the veil removed. At least I still felt like me. Betrothal changing nothing within me.

I could hear the merriment between the men as I slipped into my pallet. It had been an anxious day. At least now I knew he was not old and wrinkled. I did not know yet the interior of his heart, but this union would not guarantee that. I would have to call upon my womanly ways, but as of yet they were elusive to me.

~45~

Sister Ann

Mass concluded as the sun moved above the trees, shaping an afternoon of warm sunshine. As the sisters filed out of the chapel, each of them were off to their daily tasks. Ann lingered in the vestibule, unsure of what to do. At long last, she was greeted by Sr. Francis Xavier, who motioned that she follow her to the office.

Ann remembered being there for the first time with a shudder. She had barely arrived, still shivering from cold and fear. Her meager belongings were taken from her as she was given linen shift to wear. The rules given were very simple... do as you are told, do as you are told, and do as you are told. She thought she might be given a habit to wear immediately, but was told that for now, she would retain her worldly ways. "The commitment to the order was a process," they said.

"You must be totally sure before you take your vows, and so must we."

That had been a month ago, and now it was time to become a postulant formally. The ceremony was to take place at Sunday matins. At that time, she would receive her habit, leaving the earthly ways for about one year. After a testing time, she then would be able to take her final vows.

Asked if she could read, she replied, "Yes, a little," and was sent to Sr. Angela, who would oversee her education.

Ann hoped Sr. Angela would be available.

Session Date: 3-8-14

~46~

Sr. Ann

Postulants were forbidden to have visitors. The strict schedule created by the convent did not allow for any outside socialization. Chores, lessons, and prayer were filling the days without interruption.

Ann, or Sister Ann as she was now called, pulled upon the veil that pinched her forehead. They had cut her hair short upon receiving her habit. The small veil of the postulant perched upon her head. The pins that held it in place pressed upon her head uncomfortably.

She missed her long red hair, but accepted that it was an important commitment to the convent. She did wish that it not pinch so much. It was a great distraction as she went about her day.

My Soul's Journey Through Some Of My Past Lives
Based Upon True Lives

Immediately after mass, she reported to Sr. Angela for instruction. Reading was at the top of the list, followed by writing. Ann had some education, but by far and away nothing close to what was now being expected of her.

My Soul's Journey Through Some Of My Past Lives
Based Upon True Lives

Session Date: 3-9-14

~47~

Sr. Ann

The time passed quickly, and soon Ann was ready to take her final vows. No one from her family would attend the ceremony, as they had long forgotten her in their struggle to survive.

There were three who were to be solemnized in their marriage to God. It was a serious moment that was to be witnessed by all the nuns who served the Holy Spirit.

Sister Ann had fallen into the routine of lighting the kitchen fire every day. Her feet would slide across the stone floor silently before the sun rose. It had become a comfort for her to do so. It provided a moment of solitude not often experienced in the convent. Everything was communal and shared.

The idea of personal possessions was unheard of. There was no sense of personal space or awareness. There were no means of physical reflection. Sr. Ann had not looked into her reflection since she arrived. Now the idea of doing so seemed silly and foolish. She wondered if she had changed? Well of course, she had.

Her veil and habit hid the girl she used to be. Somehow she had become merely a vessel of experience. Her personal identity now merged with all the other sisters.

Session Date: 3-14-14

~48~

Sr. Ann

When the bells began to chime early one morning, Sr. Ann was already awake. Getting up was now a reaction instead of the desire to get up to start her day. She questioned the validity of her father's choice in sending her here.

No one had reached out to her in the long months since her arrival. She had studied well, learning quickly from Sr. Angela all she need to become a full-fledged nun. Even the hard work needed to run the convent did not bother her.

It was the notion that her life was now as it ever would be. No better. No less, just an endless walk through the stone hallways.

*My Soul's Journey Through Some Of My Past Lives
Based Upon True Lives*

Her father still bewildered her. Did he not know how much she wanted to stay with the family?

The lack of their presence was a source of deep sadness, often invading her sleep every night. She missed her sisters, brothers, and yes, her parents.

Most of all, she missed her friend Geoffrey. The memory of his lips on hers made her feel vulnerable. A warm sensation traveled through her as she relived it once again.

Would she ever have that experience again?

Of course not. Now buried within the convent walls, her chance of ever even seeing him again was remote.

Sr. Ann could hear the others beginning to stir in their cells. Lighting the morning fire was now way past due.

My Soul's Journey Through Some Of My Past Lives
Based Upon True Lives

Session Date: 3-16-14

~49~

Sr. Ann

The stone floor was cold beneath her feet. Sometimes it seemed that the cold traveled all the way up her body. It created an ache so deep, often it took hours for it to fade from her bones.

There was still a few embers from yesterday's fire that sparkled as she entered the kitchen.

"Thank the Lord," she whispered.

It meant that getting it restarted would move quickly. A few pieces of wood were still in the chest by the window, perhaps she could wait a bit before going for more wood. With any luck, the sun would be high above by that time, making the wood gathering less uncomfortable.

My Soul's Journey Through Some Of My Past Lives
Based Upon True Lives

As the fire ignited, Sr. Ann closed her eyes remembering her life before the convent. The image of Geoffrey standing before her was so vivid it felt like he was in the kitchen with her. Her body felt warm at the mere thought of him. A sense of longing filled her that was abruptly halted by the entrance of the other nuns reporting for their duties.

Sr. Ann quietly tucked away his memory, knowing she would bring it forward again at the first opportunity. She knew she was now married to God, but the thought of Geoffrey made it clear to her the decision was not a good one.

After all, she had not made this decision, her father did.

How was that fair?

In the distance Sr. Francis Xavier crossed herself as she watched Sr. Ann. Her compassion rising within heart, she waived to Sr. Ann. The girl needed reassurance and guidance. Hopefully she would feel the support that was extended in her direction.

Her heart screamed for answers, but her head knew it was futile.

With closed eyes, Sr. Francis attempted a blend. "Feel my heart. Feel my focus. All will be well."

With a sigh, she closed the chapel door. This was proving more difficult than she thought. Thankfully they had a whole life of time on their hands. With the grace of God, she would see Sr. Ann through the darkness. And she of all of them, knew how dark that could be.

Session Date: 10-23-14

~50~

Oversoul

The need to reverse the tables has led the Clare to become unbalanced in her perspective of the female energy. Supposing to create equal opportunity, resulting in the creation of a victim moment, not being able to realign quickly enough, the opportunity to experience the inequality of female has burst forward in an unfortunate event.

The twisted perspective that acting cavalier about the exchange of energy, has resulted in Clare becoming more agitated with the so-called positioning of her femaleness in another relationship.

Hopefully the moments will resolve into solution rather than a further entrenchment into aggressive behavior.

My Soul's Journey Through Some Of My Past Lives
Based Upon True Lives

Session Date: 10/06/10

~51~

Clare

"Wake up," whispered an unfamiliar voice.

The smell of sweat mixed with a spice unknown to her filled her nostrils.

It seemed like a dream in the dimly lit room. Not knowing how she got here, Clare tried to sit up. A hand pushed her back down on a hard surface, which felt like a stone floor.

"What was this place? How did she get here?"

Clare ran off in her mind the sequence of events that brought her here. None of it made sense. The last thing she remembered was a hotel room with someone handing her roses.

My Soul's Journey Through Some Of My Past Lives
Based Upon True Lives

"Oh that's right. It was her rendezvous guy. Prince Charming. Where did he go?"

The whisper came again with hot breath close to her ear. Turning, she could not make out the face but the words repeated. "Wake up."

Clare tried once again to focus to see who it was. The room was not her hotel room. There were sheer curtains throughout and what looked like an outdoor fire pit in the center.

It felt like an odd camp out with the Girl Scouts or the like.

"How did she get here?"

This was not her sterile hotel room. She must have been abducted or something. However, she felt light headed and baffled by the change of venue.

Clare put her hand to her temple trying to clear her thoughts. It was then she noticed the jewelry dangling from her wrist. It looked like diamonds and gold blended together in an intricate design.

"What the heck was this?"

She watched the bracelet twinkle in the candlelight.

"Candlelight? Where were the lamps?"

There had to be a light switch somewhere. At last her eyes began to focus and the room took shape. It looked like a tent.

"Or was it a campsite?"

The bracelet continued to distract her until she heard muffled tones approaching.

A flap of fabric revealed a man.

My Soul's Journey Through Some Of My Past Lives
Based Upon True Lives

"Should she be frightened?"

Clare squinted her eyes to see him better.

"I see you have awakened dear Hasor. Should I send for food and drink?"

The face was familiar but the dress appeared odd. She was in Chicago after all. If she was still there and it wasn't Halloween, then something was terribly wrong.

My Soul's Journey Through Some Of My Past Lives
Based Upon True Lives

Session Date: 11-11-10

~52~

Clare

Her finger tips brushed across a carpet while her cheek felt the smoothness of the pillow. An odd aroma filled her nostrils causing her head to spin. The last time she felt this way she had sipped one too many glasses of champagne. She could recall how the bubbles seemed to pop inside her mouth as the liquid poured down her throat.

That moment mixed with this, required Clare to grip the carpet to regain her stability. It was plush with soft fibers rather unlike any carpet she had felt before. There was also an odor that she could not identify. Sort of a musky smell that brought images to her mind that were unpleasant.

My Soul's Journey Through Some Of My Past Lives
Based Upon True Lives

She tried to sit up but found to her dismay that she was restrained not by ropes, but a hand that firmly gripped her waist.

The conflict of reality was disturbing. Clare called out, but to whom she was not certain.

"Would anyone hear her in the hotel? Was she still there? Or was she transported to a different place unbeknownst to her?"

All the while her hand stoked the carpet in hopes of defining what she was experiencing.

"Had she gone mad? Or was she truly a victim in the clutches of someone who would harm her?"

The pile of the carpet gave way to a stone floor that was completely unfamiliar.

"Wake up," came the whisper again. The heat of the speaker's breath felt warm upon her neck.

"Who was this person?"

Clare managed to turn her body to the side giving her the ability to glimpse her captor.

Session Date: 10-27-14

~53~

Oversoul

The aspects manifest themselves to resolve the conflicts. Each one having difficult experiences according to their perspective of the issue.

In a fleeting moment of dramatics, Clare finds herself suddenly victim in a situation she often controls. The negativity attached to it leaves her feeling vulnerable to the male energy of who she had previously dominated, or proposed that she did.

We can feel the nun called Ann in despair over the wrongs she perceived she endured from a father who viewed her as a burden. We rush to her side to find her rediscovering the woman in herself. The abandonment by her family, and most notably her father, leads her.

We decide to enlist a guide that has similar experience to Ann. In the form of a nun, she lingers in the sidelines, supporting Ann through the difficult adjustments. Without a word, the energy softens for her, the guide expertly soothing the energy.

We rejoice in the outcome, feeling that all would be well. The guide, however, felt that one will find no solace when love is unrequited. After all, Sr. Francis Xavier was of similar experience, and the impact still vivid in her consciousness.

An interesting choice, the connection between the two. We hoped for comfort during Ann's experience.

Session Date: 10-30-14

~54~

Clare

Was I being sold into slavery?

I had heard of the practice. Maybe it was very real and happening to me. My only thoughts were to escape any way that I could.

I was not shackled in any way. Certainly I could talk my way out of this madness.

He leaned in while smiling.

"Ah Hasor! You honor me with your great beauty!"

What?

My Soul's Journey Through Some Of My Past Lives
Based Upon True Lives

Who?

Good god, was this mistaken identity?

"I am not Hasor," I replied.

"Ah, but you are my sweet girl."

He took me in his arms while I thought feverishly about escape.

My Soul's Journey Through Some Of My Past Lives
Based Upon True Lives

Session Date: 10-30-14

~55~

Clare

The candles burned down as my head spun in an array of explosions. Mini explosions would be the better term I suppose.

This man continued his assault upon me, while whispering terms of endearment. It was not so much a rape, but a seduction. One that made no sense to me at all.

He spoke of our future, our sons, and the blessing of the gods upon us?

What?

His love making not gentle but deliberate, I found myself going along in case he became violent. But he didn't.

Who and what was this?

I felt myself drifting off. The fragrant surroundings becoming more comfortable. If he meant me harm, surely there would have been evidence of it by now. I had had too much experience in this department not to be able to recognize someone's intent.

At least I thought I had.

He rose from the cushions while brushing my hair from my cheek.

"Sleep now," he said softly.

My eyes were heavy and I felt myself relaxing into the comfort. Whatever this guy was up to, I would deal with it in the morning.

My Soul's Journey Through Some Of My Past Lives
Based Upon True Lives

Session Date: 10-04-10

~56~

Hasor

The blow came swiftly, before I was prepared to take it. I felt my legs buckle beneath me as my right side collided with the marble floor.

There was immense pain, but there was immunity from the repetition that numbed me.

A trickle of blood oozed from the corner of my mouth. Its salty taste revived me momentarily.

"Should I brace for more?"

A shadow passed before me as he strode from the room. Emptiness followed as I lifted my hand to wipe my mouth.

My Soul's Journey Through Some Of My Past Lives
Based Upon True Lives

"Was this the life I had awaited as a girl?"

My mother had told me of the difficulties with men. It was our duty to please and conform to their ways of living.

"It was the way of women to serve and obey, was it not?"

I could feel the bruise rising on my cheek. Seeking a cool cloth, it soothed the pulse of pain that was beginning to rise.

"Would it also calm the heart that now pulsed with fear?"

He would never apologize. It was his way to demean and humiliate.

"Was it mine to be victim?"

I did not know.

My Soul's Journey Through Some Of My Past Lives
Based Upon True Lives

I closed my eyes wishing myself away to another place. This was not what I wanted. I retreated to my inner self until it was over.

Upon return, the starry sky presented itself by the window beckoning me to forget the difficulty. Tomorrow it would be like it never was. The only reminder a purple blemish that in days would fade, to be no more.

"Was that my fate as well?"

I threw my wedding ring to the floor. No longer did I wish to be a woman.

Session Date: 11-18-4

~57~

Oversoul

The experiences overlap while creating the drama. We watch with interest as the aspects begin to feel the presence of others.

A consideration of the best outcome is one of awareness. The recognition so far has not been a detriment to the overall growth.

Should all the personalities intermingle, what would be the outcome?

We wait with anticipation as the energy unfolds. Our focus upon the Hasor remains steadfast.

Session Date: 10-31-14

~58~

Clare

The blanket felt rough on my cheek as I unconsciously pulled it to my face. It smelled like industrial laundry soup, which caused my nostrils to flare. A sense of an impending sneeze forced me to push the covers off of my body. I felt constricted even without the covers. It was then I realized I was still fully clothed.

My suit jacket was bunched uncomfortably around my shoulders. Blouse still buttoned. . . Skirt twisted around so the zipper was in the front.

I even still wore my necklace of heavy beads, which poked into my ear in a most unusual way.

My eyes flew open expecting to be still in the harem environment. Certainly my reluctant behavior of the night before would have been a problem this morning.

A small glimmer of sunlight poked into the greyness of the room. As I focused, I realized I was in my hotel room.

My hotel room?

How could that be?

Yet most definitely that's where I was. Still dressed in my business attire. Rumpled and stiff, I stumbled into the bathroom to look in the mirror.

The bright lights of the bathroom glared at me in the most unflattering way. Apparently I had not even bothered to wash my face.

"Ah Clare, are you not the most pitiful of creatures in the morning?"

My Soul's Journey Through Some Of My Past Lives
Based Upon True Lives

I was confused.

The events of last evening still ran vividly in my mind.

I had come into the room. Someone had been there. Was it not the Prince Charming of the night before?

I simply was not sure.

The memory of being taken to another place. (Don't they call that kidnapping?) Held against my will? Assaulted by a man who acted like a lover?

It happened.

I know it did.

But. . .

My Soul's Journey Through Some Of My Past Lives
Based Upon True Lives

Here the evidence says, I slept in my clothes, did not wash my face, and no evidence of anyone else being there.

It was strange.

I slipped off my clothes and jumped into the shower. The heat rejuvenating my disgruntled body wonderfully. My mind retraced the previous evening with great detail.

My past and my present were not coinciding.

Was I drunk?

No.

Was I drugged somehow?

No.

Did I feel violated?

My Soul's Journey Through Some Of My Past Lives
Based Upon True Lives

Oddly, yes.

I must have been drunk and passed out.

Yes that was it.

Then I remembered the man kept referring to me as "Hasor," or something like that.

Then I remembered. . . Clearly.... I had only a glass of wine.

What the hell was happening?

My Soul's Journey Through Some Of My Past Lives
Based Upon True Lives

1 Session Date: 1-04-14

~59~

Clare

Stumbling into the bathroom, the glaring lights blinded me to the first glimpses of myself. Mascara down my nose, and topped off with dark circle puffiness under each eye.

I reached for a wash cloth, allowing the faucet to run into its hottest flow. Placed upon my face, I felt a surge of life coming back into my body. I felt no worse for wear, but uncomfortable in my now wrinkled suit.

What had happened?

Apparently what I thought had happened did not. There was no evidence of attack. No ripped clothing, only a dull dryness in my mouth that needed water as soon as possible.

My Soul's Journey Through Some Of My Past Lives
Based Upon True Lives

Session Date: 9-12-15

~60~

Clare

I fell back asleep for a while. My body felt exhausted. The vivid memories of last night were confusing. Maybe it was all a dream after all. Disturbing as it was, the facts were that I was indeed just fine. I felt hung over, but I knew there had been no huge amounts of alcohol consumed.

Fortunately this morning of sleep was dreamless. No mysterious lover, no nameless Prince Charming lurking in the shadows of my hotel room. At least he left without any muss or fuss. I must have just been overly tired, and passed out as soon as I got back.

The dream, however, lingered with me. It was so detailed that I still could smell the heavy fragrance of the place. Flowers of some sort, yes flowers. I stood in the bathroom trying to identify the flowers.

Jasmine.

Yes the fragrance was Jasmine. It certainly did not smell like that now in this hotel room. That was some wild dream.

I moved about trying to gather all my belongings. I had the strong desire to leave and head home. My thoughts of looking for some hookup now felt empty. The sooner I could get out of here, the better.

Checkout time had been at 11 AM. It was way past that time, but I found myself not even caring if I had to pay for an extra day. The need to leave was so strong I just threw everything into my suitcase.

On my way out the door, my eye caught a glimmer of gold in the carpet. Thinking I had dropped an earring, I stooped down to retrieve it. To

my surprise it was indeed a circular ring of gold.
Could be an earring or the like, but it certainly
wasn't mine. What was curious was that it was
engraved with symbols that I didn't recognize.

It was indeed a ring-like piece of jewelry. Not
your run of the mill costume jewelry. Looked
expensive. I slipped it on my finger, feeling
transfixed by the perfect way it fit my finger.

The smell of Jasmine washed over me in a wave.
Was this some sort of déjà vu?

Ridiculous! Time to gather my belongings and
get out of here. Too many vivid experiences in one
day for this girl.

Looking at the ring on my finger was disturbing
because I felt somehow attached to it. Whoever
dropped it here must be looking for it. I would leave
it at the front desk on my way out.

My Soul's Journey Through Some Of My Past Lives
Based Upon True Lives

Session Date: 10-1-15

~61~

Oversoul

Decision to take a more male roll

Clare arrived quietly into a world that did not provide the ability to create her deepest desire.

As we observed disappointment upon disappointment with her ideal feminine purpose, there was an emptiness that presented itself.

Feeling vulnerable within her felinity during her early years, Clare developed a dominant more masculine approach when dealing with male/female relationships. In this way, she became the one in power. The one who decided who mattered, and who did not. The helplessness of Sr. Ann and Mary left her focused upon not accepting victimhood in

My Soul's Journey Through Some Of My Past Lives
Based Upon True Lives

any manner.   Unfortunately, it created a harsh outlook that actually was all consuming.

Session Date: 9-13-15

~62~

Mary

So during my lunch I glanced about the office to see if a small amount of privacy might be available. This website about past lives needed a terse response for their aggressive assault upon my work computer. Hopefully there would be a contact email or phone number where I could lodge a complaint.

I did not appreciate the intrusion. If it kept up, my office manager would no doubt reprimand me if it continued. I did not ask for their contact. The idea of other lives was extremely foreign to me. I was not raised with that kind of nonsense. Mom and Dad were not all that religious, so my beliefs were rather average. There was one life. You gave it your best shot, died, and went to whatever the afterlife offered. The idea of many lives made me

queasy. One was more than enough. No need for
multiple ones.

As soon as it looked safe, I pulled up this
website. Whoever ran it was going to get a piece of
my mind. The aggressive advertising was an
attribute of the Internet I deplored. So here it was:
"Past Lives".

There was not a phone number, only an email
address for the sole purpose of getting so-called past
life readings. Really? That seemed so lame to not
have an official contact number. Well, not to be
deterred, I composed a terse email presenting my
objections to their rude advertising.

I cited this Hasor person for being intrusive.
How in the world did she know my name? It was
uncomfortable to say the least, and who knew if it
was male or female?

The faster I typed, the more irritated I became. I
felt a bit calmer when I finished. Whoever received

it, would no doubt not answer. Most of these outfits were shady enterprises. At least I had had my say and hopefully I would be bothered no further.

Lunch was drawing to a close while I was typing, which left me with no opportunity to eat. At least a cup of tea could fuel me until I could get some food. Maybe someone would have some cookies squirreled away in their desk.

I went to the staff kitchen to make some tea. Luckily there was one bag of Jasmine tea left. Lucky me! At least I would have that comfort.

The rest of the day flew by. I was buried in the paperwork that was piled on my desk continually. It felt like a huge avalanche that could never be finished. Digging my heels in, I typed up all the contracts and revisions that were handed to me. My job seemed endless. It was 5 o'clock when I finally looked up.

My Soul's Journey Through Some Of My Past Lives
Based Upon True Lives

There was a lot still to do, but I felt relieved that I at least put a dent in it.

As everyone was leaving, I decided to check email one more time. The letter to the website was not even in my thoughts anymore. I had vented my frustration, so I felt good.

"You've Got Mail."

Hopefully there were no new assignments for me. I would skim through them because I wanted to go home without the added stress.

Dave tapped my desk as he was leaving. "Hope your computer is holding," he said with a smile.

"Oh yes, it's great," I replied.

My eyes watched him get on the elevator with a wave. Anxious to follow him, I glanced through the new emails from this afternoon.

My Soul's Journey Through Some Of My Past Lives
Based Upon True Lives

Info from Past Lives?

The idea that this site would reply sent a small shiver down my back. Surely it was some automated response.

"Dear Miss Mary,

We received your complaint regarding the intrusive advertisement on the Internet. We assure you that our company is of the highest integrity. Aggressive emails and unwanted pop-ups are not part of our interaction with the general public. Only those who request information are contacted personally by our staff. While we do advertise, we assure you that it is a banner approach placed in the classified sections that are designated on the Internet. In no way would any practitioner or employee contact you in an unsolicited manner.

We hope you have resolved these issues from your end. Perhaps your computer has been tampered with or someone is involved in creating a prank of some sort.

Also, we do not have, nor have we had anyone in our employ by the name of Hasor.

Sincerely,
Margret Olsen"

Session Date: 9-16-15

~63~

Mary

The hands of the office clock continued to make time. The multiple fragrances of perfume from those who passed by my desk on their journey home, drifted into a foggy atmosphere. I was alone, reading the email that basically informed me that I did not have a clear grasp of my senses. Of course they would say that! They had to have many complaints such as mine! Irritated, I turned off my computer to go home.

The more I thought about it, the more angry I became. Why did I get an email from someone called Hasor! It just didn't make sense. Realizing I might still have the email, I checked my inbox. Alas, it was nowhere to be found.

My Soul's Journey Through Some Of My Past Lives
Based Upon True Lives

Too tired to pursue it more, I gathered my belongings to go home. Anyone who got involved with past life hocus pocus, was either raving mad, or criminal. In this case, I would say criminal. Imagine having to resort to these tactics to trick people into participating in your business! Tomorrow I would compose a reply to let "Past Lives" know that I was on to them.

Tomorrow was a new day. I would find that email as proof of their intention.

I hated being called a liar, which was essentially what they were doing.

Mumbling to myself, I stepped out onto the busy street. A sudden billow of exhaust from a passing bus caused a cough to emerge from my throat. The cement burned slightly through my shoes, making my walk to the subway miserable. Just a few more steps and I would be there at last!

My Soul's Journey Through Some Of My Past Lives
Based Upon True Lives

I settled into a seat, only to look up into the face of a small billboard about one of those cheap psychics one reads about. Her talents included clairvoyance, Tarot Cards, and of course, Past Lives. I just couldn't catch a break!

Soon, I was putting my keys in the lock at home. I sat down my purse, scaring my kitty in the process.

"Here Jasmine! Come back! I'm so sorry."

With a bit of coaching, she peered out to me with a small meow.

"Sorry sweetie!" I picked her up feeling the warmth of her deep purr.

My Soul's Journey Through Some Of My Past Lives
Based Upon True Lives

Session Date: 9-17-15

~64~

Mary

My living room was a comfortable space. Decorating was not my greatest strength, but I managed to create a semblance of home within it. My cat and I immediately nestled into the deep seated sofa. The stress of the day slowly disintegrated as I stroked soft fur beneath my fingers.

Oh! If it could always be this comforting. Laying my head against the well cushioned arm, the calmness finally began to envelope me.

All of this turmoil with this website was keeping my nerves in an agitated state. Actually, I had heard of past lives here and there, equating it with the

My Soul's Journey Through Some Of My Past Lives
Based Upon True Lives

hocus pocus of a carnival circus. Certainly no one took that nonsense seriously.

My family was very conservative with their religious beliefs. One life, one death, and then off to heaven or hell you went. Everything else considered nonsense.

Now, that nonsense could creep into anyone's life. The Internet offered an ability to sneak into someone's life without any protection. The fact that this Past Life place could intrude into my life this way was disturbing.

I simply was not interested. Perhaps they thought by addressing me by my first name it would trick me into trusting them. Well they were wrong. I never would accept all that gibberish about multiple lives. Simply nonsense.

My alarm went off again too early. I had never left the couch. My cat and I were cuddled tightly together when I heard the alarm ringing in my room.

My Soul's Journey Through Some Of My Past Lives
Based Upon True Lives

Stumbling into the bedroom, I managed to turn it off quickly. Still in my work clothes from the night before, I shook my finger at my reflection in the bathroom mirror.

"We have to stop meeting like thi!" The girl reflected back at me looked rumpled and tired. What was the point to all of this anyway? Splashing cold water on my face did not prompt an answer from me. All I really wanted to do was go back to the couch and sleep.

Session Date: 9-18-15

~65~

Mary

The one friend I had who had known me since we were kids left me a message during lunch. For some reason I did not pick it up till much later.

Her name was Sue Hutch. We met in the third grade. She had beaten me in the yearly spelling bee. We were rivals, but we became fast friends. Both of us were outcasts of sorts. Not that popular, not that pretty, not so athletic. We were, however, great competitors in academics. Seeking solace in each other, I believe we survived Middle School, Junior, and Senior High because of our friendship.

We went in different directions after high school, not intersecting again until our late 20's. By then we were both convinced that we would be old maids together. Suzie made me smile, and for that she had my external gratitude.

Her voice mail announced her impending arrival in the city. Her usual mandatory dinner and girl time at the top of her agenda. I eagerly returned the call, hopeful her arrival would be imminent.

"I will be there tomorrow," she said as soon as she heard my voice.

"Great!" I replied. "Of course we will have our mandatory dinner. Please tell me you will spend the night at my place. I have a story to tell you that just can't wait!"

"Meet you at your office at 5," she replied. "Then I am yours!"

The news felt great. I really needed to talk with someone who knew and cared about me!

When we hung up, I found myself counting the hours until we would rendezvous. Somehow work went more smoothly in my anticipation of her impending arrival.

My Soul's Journey Through Some Of My Past Lives
Based Upon True Lives

Session Date: 10-25-14

~66~

Oversoul

The path of choice in each of the experiences becomes tedious for the incarnate. Our focus, to ease the tension felt, never appears to be sufficient.

In an effort to evolve, each one in her own way strives for achievement. Our namesake Hasor teeters on the edge of the balance necessary to create a complete awareness, only to stumble recklessly as Clare and Sister Ann. A victim of circumstance? Or a creator of an environment dedicated to abstinence for her own contemplation?

As the lives evolve, it is easy to assume they, like the linear, come one after other. Realistically, they happen simultaneously for a complete energy circle.

HASOR

My Soul's Journey Through Some Of My Past Lives
Based Upon True Lives

Now we focus in another aspect of the total. The goal still the same with different dramatics. We guide the vibration so that all is included in the total picture.

Our thoughts linger with each of them.

My Soul's Journey Through Some Of My Past Lives
Based Upon True Lives

Session Date: 3-20-14

~67~

Sr. Ann

The years began to move quickly past her. Each day filled with chapel, prayer, and more prayer. The convent had been good as far as the care of the body, but Ann's soul yearned for more. The image of Geoffrey never far from her thoughts.

"I wonder what the world would be like if I had been able to keep kissing Geoffrey?"

"Would he have asked for my hand in marriage?"

"Would my father have consented?"

All these thoughts invaded her thoughts daily. A piece of her still lingered outside of the high stone walls that surrounded her. She tried to be a good nun, doing all the tasks that were asked of her with a pure heart. In the cobwebbed corners of her heart, the idea of motherhood also haunted her.

To hold a child in your arms was something that would never be hers. At least, not in this life.

Of course that was not the perspective she was supposed to have. It was important to live your life, your one life, as close to God as possible. Of course she was consecrated to God, so that had to be good news. At least that is what she was told.

My Soul's Journey Through Some Of My Past Lives
Based Upon True Lives

Session Date: 3-21-14

~68~

Sr. Ann

"I stand in the chapel seeking solace from the ache in my heart. Years of living virtually with only my rosary for comfort, gives me pause as to the why of my circumstance.

Yes, I have received wisdom, food, lodging, and the spirit of our dear Lord, but the ever filled day of devotion left no moments for living. It has been many years since my father left me upon the stone steps of this convent, and emotion and attention to a young girl that had essentially been ripped from her family to this day leaves me bewildered."

"As I pray I notice the dark spots upon my calloused hands. The fingernails chipped from the

My Soul's Journey Through Some Of My Past Lives
Based Upon True Lives

kitchen work that is my contribution to the sisterhood."

"How many times have my feet felt the coldness of the stone floors before sun would rise?"

"So many prayers and sacrifices for the benefit of the community. How does one feel so alone in the midst of so many?"

"If only the morning of my family departure had been different. What would have transpired if I had had the courage to say no?"

"I have often dreamed of a different unfolding where I walked to the end of the lane in defiance. Seeking Geoffrey to tell him of the plan to secret me away to a life that should have enacted itself."

"So I stand now in the chapel asking the God from above, why?"

"Why did it unfold this way? My skin sags on the bones that often ache in misery. It has been a lifetime shut away. No one ever so much as inquired about my wellbeing. I suppose they feel that I am in the hands of God."

The wind gently blows through the arches of the sacristy. Through a small window I can see an apple tree in full spring bloom. Soon I would be boiling the apples to make a sweet potage for all to enjoy. A small contribution and privilege for the sisters who have kept this institution alive for so long.

I wish it had been different. So many moments never to become an experience for me. Phantom children that only exist in my mind run up and down the cloister hall. If I listen carefully I can almost hear their laughter.

They should have been my children. The ability to choose, taken away so soon and so young.

Session Date: 3-22-14

~69~

Sr. Ann

Sr. Ann wiped a tear from her eye as she knelt in the chapel. In the distance she could hear the other sisters speaking amongst themselves. It must be time for the evening meal. The sun was lower leaving her feel the day had slipped away as well as her life.

She should be about her duties. There were places to sit, food to be served, and ale to be drank.

The well was about dry, so water had to be carried from the creek. The need to drink it less than the need to cook with it. The ale was the safest drinking water in the whole area. The sisters made

My Soul's Journey Through Some Of My Past Lives
Based Upon True Lives

their own with the barley that was grown in the fields. A source of income as well.

It took a great effort for Sr. Ann to get up those days from her kneeling at the altar. Time and the stone floors had taken their toll.

HASOR

My Soul's Journey Through Some Of My Past Lives
Based Upon True Lives

Session Date: 3-25-14

~70~

Sr. Ann

Retrospect

I should be feeling the hand of God upon me. For so many years my service has been consistent, while keeping the thoughts of a different life at bay.

Where did the days go?

Along with my hope, they vanished somewhere between chapel and the kitchen fire. The tasks completed to the satisfaction of my superiors, I still stumbled in my desire to have a different life.

Long have I been resistant to losing hope in this life of solitude. It was not what I envisioned. It was not the fulfillment of my desires.

My Soul's Journey Through Some Of My Past Lives
Based Upon True Lives

Though the convent was full of sisters, there was no real intimacy. There was never enough time to talk or become close to anyone.

There was a sister Francis that had brought comfort just with her eyes. She had long ago went to her heavenly father. Oddly, I missed her. She had taken a vow of silence, but always had a smile for me. Often just the touch of her hand could soothe me.

When she died, I grieved for weeks. Something about her was different. I was never sure what it was, but I liked her quite a bit.

Sadly, she had left me here to live out this life on my own. I hoped to see her again when I left this body.

Closing my eyes, I grieve for the loss of Geoffrey. His kiss still lingers in my thoughts. His breath upon my cheek still fresh to this day.

My Soul's Journey Through Some Of My Past Lives
Based Upon True Lives

The chapel bells chime in harmony with my heart. Yet the discord of disappointment leaves me tearful in regret.

To this day, I have no awareness of why this life was chosen for me. Did my father know the travesty he created? Or did he simply continue with survival, hoping I would forget my wishes?

I am certain his life has long ago ended, for no word of him has ever reached me. The family I loved and knew never reached into the convent for news of my life. The constant whispers of their voices visit me in my dreams, as the lonely moments continue within these stone walls.

I only now wish for the touch of Geoffrey, who most certainly has forgotten my name.

Session Date: 4-3-14

~71~

Sr. Ann

While I sat alone with God in this place of stone, I questioned the truth of why it turned out to be this way.

Alone in my cell, I wait for the sun to begin to peek out from behind the hill. Long has it been since I lit the morning fire. Feeble hands have difficulty lighting fires on cold mornings. My hands surprise me in their feebleness. I so thought to be young forever. A misconception of the young often brought to bear in later times.

I feel the youth in my heart as I kiss again the lips of Geoffrey, if only in my memory.

No children. No husband. No family to embrace my lonely heart. I have been told that my husband is God, but it feels lonely in this marriage.

I like to dream that he waited for the return of my person so that he could truly be with his love. Maybe he never married. Maybe he pined for my presence while suffering a life of celibacy like I did. Would the truth of my plight surprise him in this day?

Surely he has long forgotten, but I rather like to believe of his longing. Perhaps he never married, never was happy, or never kissed a girl since that moment.

Yes. That's what I would render the perfect outcome, however, my wits know the story.

A young man such as he would have gone on to a houseful of children. All of them eager to embrace Papa at the end of each day.

My Soul's Journey Through Some Of My Past Lives
Based Upon True Lives

Session Date: 4-7-14

~72~

Sr. Ann

Should I have another chance?

The fires of passion have lingered in my body all these years. Only a small memory of fulfillment fills my thoughts. If I had run away, would I be scorned, or would I have been blessed?

O' how wretched my life has been while praying to a merciful God. There has been no pity for this woman's heart. Per chance another chance? Alas no. With only one path carried out by my father do I remain pure, but not content.

I know the blood in my veins has slowed in the past years. Something has weakened my gait as I walk to mass each day. I know I should be grateful

My Soul's Journey Through Some Of My Past Lives
Based Upon True Lives

and of good cheer for the life I've had as a good sister, but I remain saddened, never to have been a true woman in this life.

What would it have been like?

My thoughts run rampant with pictures, but to no avail. Removed I am from a life I sought now that opportunity alludes me.

I await death as a release from the shackles of routine. If heaven awaits me then I go willingly, but again, not without regrets.

I should thank my father, but I cannot. I die estranged from his alleged indifference.

My Soul's Journey Through Some Of My Past Lives
Based Upon True Lives

Session Date: 4-16-14

~73~

Sr. Ann

I would have been more resistant to the prayer times. The quiet of the stone rooms make way daily to the connection I seek. If they be not of physical, the hope of the presence of angels fill my thoughts.

Are the fluttering wings the sound that gives a lullaby to my sleeping hours? Or are all the noises merely an imaginative recital of my own beliefs?

I am one with God, for it has been required of me. Is this of truth?

I only know of its requirement.

The legitimacy of the union escapes me as I ponder my life.

HASOR

My Soul's Journey Through Some Of My Past Lives
Based Upon True Lives

I conclude that had the choice been mine, there would not have been a convent or other spiritual house. The house would have been mine. Filled with laughing children instead of halls that echoed silence.

The lateness of the hour decides for me. I lay my quill down satisfied that I have spoken freely. For this freedom has long escaped me.

I retire to my cell... alone... or am I?

The ghost of Geoffrey in my thoughts fills me with regret. I release it for the return I know will come.

Time to go to the Lord. I know it but I retreat under my coverlet, hoping for a reprieve. The moment upon me, I move towards the light, perhaps a connection will be there waiting to alleviate my loneliness.

HASOR

My Soul's Journey Through Some Of My Past Lives
Based Upon True Lives

Oh father, what have you done?

My Soul's Journey Through Some Of My Past Lives
Based Upon True Lives

Session Date: 4-26-14

~74~

Sr. Ann

The peach tree blossoms came early that spring. Their fragrance was a lingering moment in the air, when one passed by the tree. The good sisters always were grateful for the years that bore fruit for all to enjoy. It was not every year, but this summer there was sure to be fruit.

The tree was visible from the entry way into the cloister. Sr. Ann had followed the fragrance to the door frame where she held tightly. Her balance not up to her walking freely, she did manage to move slowly to be able to see the blossoms of said peach tree.

A young postulant stood a few feet behind her, ready to catch her if she fell. Her insistence to be mobile, a well know endeavor. The sisters now stood ready to assist her knowing it futile to try to stop her from her will to still live freely.

Her feet were weak, but her heart was strong. Her worn hands clenched the stone wall in the indentions of fallen pebbles. Her eyes glistening in appreciation for this wondrous spring gift.

She knew it was the last peach blossoms she would see, thus making her all the more determined to be standing there on this fine morning.

Sr. Ann has spent the last 60 years within these stone walls. Everything she needed was here, or so it seemed. Never had she ventured beyond the walls that had held her against her true will for all this time. Dedicated herself to God, it had not been her choice. A fact that she shared freely with anyone who would listen. Now being an older member of the sisterhood, she constantly had met each new postulant with anticipation, hoping to glean any opportunity to find out what was happening in the outside world.

News of her family would trickle in from time to time. Her father had passed on some years back. She had hoped he would return to see her at some point, but he never did.

Neither did any of her family. It was if a thick door had closed with no one having a key to make an entrance. If Geoffrey had lived, died, married, divorced, or breathed, it was not available.

Her heart ached with loss.

My Soul's Journey Through Some Of My Past Lives
Based Upon True Lives

Session Date: 5-7-14

~75~

Sr. Ann

The sun peeked over the walls, heralding another day. Sr. Ann slowly pulled herself up from her cot, blinking her eyes rapidly to focus them. Today was a feast day of the unification. There were many things to prepare in the chapel, so she quickly donned her veil and sandals. Her habit was worn, but sturdy against the morning chill. Kitchen duties had long been given to other nuns still agile with youth. Sister Ann could no longer bear the up keep and strenuous chores. She rather missed the hustle bustle of the morning, but found that prayer and devotion in the chapel was easier on her brittle bones.

This morning she stopped to pick some daisies in the garden to put upon the alter. There was to be a celebratory mass followed by some music to celebrate the announcement of the coming birth of Christ.

While shading her eyes, the daisies came into focus. Bending down to pick them was cumbersome, but she knelt down anyway. On her knees, they were easier to pick. Several bouquets would be needed, so Sr. Ann spread her apron to carry them all.

At first she did not hear the whisper of her name. Her ears often played tricks on her these days so she did not even look up at first.

Sister Ann? Sister Ann?

There it was again. She looked behind her only to see the other nuns going in and out of the kitchen with chores.

Sister Ann?

Slowly Sr. Ann pulled herself up to her feet. Who was this person?

Why were they whispering?

Feeling annoyed, her gaze slowly examined the garden.

No one.

How odd?

"Sr. Ann." There it was again.

As she tried to focus her eyes, a hand touched her shoulder. It startled her as she turned around.

"Who are you?"

In the same moment, there was no need for an answer. Indeed there was a someone there. It was an old man, slightly stooped with age. At first he seemed a stranger, but as he looked into her eyes she realized who he was.

Geoffrey.

"I've come to fetch you," he said, his eyes twinkling the same as they had all those years ago.

Beside him stood Sr. Francis Xavier, smiling with great love at the two of us.

"All is now as it should be," she said out loud.

Surprised, I hugged her realizing that she had guided me well all those years. The one true energy that held empathy for my situation.

My Soul's Journey Through Some Of My Past Lives
Based Upon True Lives

Session Date: 5-10-14

~76~

Sr. Ann

His eyes embraced her as she moved towards him. It was odd to see him so close after all these years. Sr. Ann had not looked into her reflection since she had entered the convent. It never had occurred to her in all these years to take notice of how she looked. Suddenly she was aware of her body. Had she changed? Did he still see her as the young maid that she was? So long ago?

Her hair now short, was tucked away under her veil. Her habit hung loosely upon her fragile body. Was it sinful to now be so aware of herself?

His eyes danced with appreciation, allowing her to relax a little. Why was he here?

My Soul's Journey Through Some Of My Past Lives
Based Upon True Lives

How did he ever get in?

All these thoughts raced through her mind. Geoffrey continued towards her. Would they embrace?

Sr. Ann was filled with anticipation and fear.

"I've come to take you home," he whispered.

Sr. Francis with her beau and I with my Geoffrey glided easily through the stone walls. The immense freedom feeling normal and quite right.

I felt the others and knew we all were playing our parts that would not diminish. The loneliness, despair, and the unanswered questions all resolved in the prism-like spectacle before me.

My Soul's Journey Through Some Of My Past Lives
Based Upon True Lives

Session Date: 5-13-14

~77~

Sr. Ann

Ann wanted to believe it was true. She felt her heart lurch in her chest as it began to flutter in the final efforts of breathing. Her hands clinched at her sides while she stood transfixed upon Geoffrey. He looked the same. His dimpled cheeks surround the brightness of his smile. Oh how she had missed that smile.

With great effort she stepped forward into her future. Life in the convent blending into oblivion behind her. The smell of Jasmine filled her nostrils, giving her a sense of euphoria. Her fingers touched the fabric of his waistcoat. It felt very fine, very fine indeed. Perhaps Geoffrey had done well for himself. A man now of means who no longer needed his father's permission to court the woman he loved.

My Soul's Journey Through Some Of My Past Lives
Based Upon True Lives

"I should tell mother Agnes that I am leaving", she whispered.

His eyes grew soft as he said, "she already knows."

With that, he grasped her hand.

Sr. Francis Xavier smiled as they moved into the mist of eternity. Her task complete, she turned to her Andrew and kissed him.

Session Date: 5-16-14

~78~

Sr. Ann
(Oversoul)

The convent faded away as they walked into the void. United within their energy, the pre-existing definitions no longer mattered.

They were one again under the umbrella of simple energy. The previous incarnation receding with the availability of connection.

It had not gone as planned. Ann and Geoffrey failed in the attempt to sustain a viable physical experience that would have allowed great growth in their relationship to themselves and each other.

In all experiences there can and will be other players who may circumvent success of the planned initiative. In the most recent, the father of Ann, due to worry of maintenance, made the decision to abdicate the opportunity set up of continuance between Geoffrey and Ann. Of course, there could have been resistance, however, the couples were not offered alternatives of behavior to remedy the situation.

This leaves both of them at a standstill regarding their progress. The awareness of Geoffrey to seek reunion was not shared by Ann, who had accepted the situation by making no movement to leave the convent. Her lack of self-esteem was exaggerated by the convent environment and the previous lack of communication within the family unit.

With the arrival of Sr. Francis, some of the distress was soothed. A new beginning of opportunity presents itself to both Ann and Geoffrey. Again with the assistance of Sr. Francis, a new experience can heal the dramatics of this experience.

My Soul's Journey Through Some Of My Past Lives
Based Upon True Lives

Session Date: 9-20-15

~79~

Mary

Sue and I embraced with energy of two women who knew each other well. It felt incredible to smell her perfume during our massive hug. All of the daily nonsense melted away as we sat on my sofa with glasses of Chardonnay.

She beguiled me with stories of her adventures with life and men. Much more aggressive than I, her tactics were often of great comedic value to me.

We never made it out for dinner, settling upon a questionable pizza from my freezer. I found some extra cheese while she rescued some sausage from the recesses of my refrigerator. Laughing hysterically, we spread the sausage and some gouda that was found upon the work of art pizza. It was a

My Soul's Journey Through Some Of My Past Lives
Based Upon True Lives

thirty minute wait, which induced us to refresh our wine. Sitting back on my couch with time in tow, we continued our assessment of the world we knew.

Hers was a long litany of men who did not work out. Mine was a quick look at the monotony of life ending with the latest mishap of the Past Life company.

I thought for sure Sue would throw her hands up in despair about this story. Least of all, the email scam from this Hasor person. Surprisingly, she was attentive while listening to my absurd story.

I showed her the email response, waiting for her usual "What kind of idiot are you?" response. Instead, Sue became quiet. There was a gathering thought look that I had not seen in a very long time.

"So, what do ya think?" I queried. She took a sip of wine before responding.

"I think there can be such things as past lives."

My Soul's Journey Through Some Of My Past Lives
Based Upon True Lives

There it was, plain and simple. My dearest of all friends just admitted, albeit backhandedly, that she ascribed to the possibility of past lives.

My throat constricted a little as I assimilated this new information.

"Why have you never said something like this before?" I asked incredulously.

"It just never came up," she replied.

"I have been dabbling in past life information for years. Never mentioned it because I though you would think I had gone weird on you!"

We both looked at each other with new awareness. It never occurred to me that my current dealings would be something my friend would know about.

Past lives?

My Soul's Journey Through Some Of My Past Lives
Based Upon True Lives

Who does that?

Apparently my best friend did. It was like a dam had burst. Sue came forth with all her experiences. It was purely amazing to me. After she finished her monologue of detail concerning her past lives, of course some of them involved yours truly. Although an equal part of them did not.

The clock chimed 10 PM, often the time I would turn in for the night. Feeling charged up, I realized that sleep would be elusive this night.

My Soul's Journey Through Some Of My Past Lives
Based Upon True Lives

Session Date: 9-20-15

~80~

Mary

We stayed up way too late. The conversation was mesmerizing. While Sue did think the contact from someone named "Hasor" was very strange, she also had heard of the website.

"Listen, past lives are very valid," she said. "I have studied this stuff quite thoroughly. I've had readings. I feel quite fond of my other selves."

At first I was shocked, but as Sue rambled on, I felt myself wondering what my past lives were. There was, however, a quarrel between that fantasy side and my logical side. I was still outraged at the inappropriate contact. The idea of past lives now made a bit more personable by my dear friend.

My Soul's Journey Through Some Of My Past Lives
Based Upon True Lives

It was decided that the Instant Message was most likely a marketing scheme gone bad. What other explanation was there?

Sue stretched out on my couch with a yawn.

"We are both going to regret this evening tomorrow morning."

I had to agree with her. Stumbling to my room, I found my cat already fast asleep. Sliding in next to her, I drifted off immediately. Visions of past lives that Sue had mentioned filled my thoughts. With only 4 hours till my alarm went off, I wondered if I could escape into one of those lives to get more sleep.

My Soul's Journey Through Some Of My Past Lives
Based Upon True Lives

Session Date: 9-21-15

~81~

Mary

Both Sue and I stumbled out of bed to face our work days. It was a harsh awakening at best. Somehow we managed to leave the apartment somewhat on time, with the promise to meet after work. It was going to be a very long day. My throbbing head a stern reminder not to drink too much and stay up late on a work night.

The day was like any other. The only difference was my headache that finally vacated midmorning. I was still left with a hollow nauseous feeling in the pit of my stomach. Fortunately work was a bit more quiet today. Anticipation of spending more time with Sue kept my spirits up despite my physical woes.

My Soul's Journey Through Some Of My Past Lives
Based Upon True Lives

I did not feel compelled to follow through with my plan to contact Past Lives. Sue had quieted my anger enough that I thought perhaps to waste no more time on it.

Besides, tonight was going to be a great time with my friend. It wasn't often that I had plans like everyone else. The clock struck five, as I pushed the elevator button. I felt slightly important as the doors closed. My friend Sue and I had a date that was just about to begin. Filled with anticipation, I splurged by hailing a cab. The restaurant was uptown, and I did not feel like taking the subway or bus. It was one of Sue's favorite places. Having never been there, the choice of a cab was a sound one. Extravagant yes! However, a smart choice.

I pulled up in front of Franco's Eatery just as my friend arrived at the entrance. Shouting my arrival, she stopped and waited for me with a huge smile.

"How did your day go?" she asked. Before I could reply she tapped her head with a grimace.

"As good as mine I presume?"

We both groaned with kindred acknowledgement of our not so great day. The good news was that it was over, and we had a whole new evening of fun awaiting us.

"A little hair of the dog," she said, as she perused the wine selections.

""Oh! I'm not so sure," I replied.

"Nonsense!" she said with authority.

"We will have a nice Merlot to toast our friendship! And the multitude of past lives that seem to be awaiting your attention!"

We both laughed, but inside I still felt a bit odd about the whole episode. All of it was just silly. I did not believe in all this stuff, although I know Sue

My Soul's Journey Through Some Of My Past Lives
Based Upon True Lives

was brimming with hope that I would at least consider it.

The waiter poured our wine into beautiful stemware. I was relaxed and happy for the first time in a while. Sue on the other hand, could not stop talking about past lives.

Apparently she was more into it than she previously let on.

"You know, I think we should get a reading done for the two of us," she said, sipping her wine.

"Maybe we have known each other before? Maybe this Hasor was a spirit reaching across the veil to contact you!"

The waiter was ready for our order and we were not ready. I fumbled for the menu while seeking a bit more time. He was a personable young man with a cute smile. I couldn't help but flush a bit when he said he would be right back.

My Soul's Journey Through Some Of My Past Lives
Based Upon True Lives

"He is way too young for you!" whispered Sue. "And besides, maybe you both have Karmic issues from another life," she added.

"Oh stop it! Will you?" I tried to hit her with my menu, but all I succeeded in doing was almost toppling her wine glass.

"Just kidding," she laughed. We ordered dinner while we continued to reminisce, giggle, and yes, considered a past life reading. By the end of the first bottle of wine, I felt good enough to consider anything.

Our waiter continued to be attentive. Making our meal a wonderful experience.

Towards the end of the evening, he overheard Sue in her quest to get me to agree to this so-called reading.

My Soul's Journey Through Some Of My Past Lives
Based Upon True Lives

"Oh, I so believe in past lives," he exclaimed. I think I was an Egyptian slave, or perhaps a Pharaoh."

I couldn't contain myself with the reply of, "Oh, I bet you were," We all laughed as he cleared our table. "Could I get you ladies coffee, tea, or an aperitif?"

Before we could reply, he looked me directly in the eye and said, "I bet you could use some Jasmine tea about now, couldn't you?"

Wide eyed I replied, "How did you know I liked Jasmine tea?"

"Oh, we slaves always know what our mistresses want."

Winking, he strode away, only to return with 2 cups of piping hot Jasmine tea. It was indeed just what I needed.

My Soul's Journey Through Some Of My Past Lives
Based Upon True Lives

"Obviously he's waited upon your every need before," whispered Sue.

"Yeah right," I laughed.

Session Date: 9-22-15

~82~

Mary

When Sue and I arrived home, we were both so tired we fell asleep immediately. It was after all, a Friday with no work on the horizon. Sue had decided to extend her stay thru Sunday, which we thought would give us permission to stay up late again. Alas, neither of us could keep our eyes open, thus sleep it was.

Sue did manage to tease me more about the waiter and to continue her pursuit of a "reading" for me. I was too tired to argue at that point, so I gave her rather sloppy permission to go ahead and book one.

Morning came too quickly. My inner clock was still in work mode. I was the first to awaken (or so I thought). Stumbling out of my room, I found Sue already wide awake at her computer. I envied her energy. She was typing furiously without noticing me.

I moved past her to the kitchen, as the only thing that would get me up and running was hot tea. Fortunately, I still had a lot left. As a good hostess, I made Sue a cup as well. When I returned to the living room, Sue threw her head up in victory with a huge "YES!!"

"Yes what!" I replied.

"Yes, you and I have an appointment with a hypnotherapist who does past life readings today at 1:00 PM! Can you believe it?"

I had to sit down while sipping my tea. Taking in Sue this early hour with all her enthusiasm was way beyond what I was used to. Trying to catch up with her was beyond me at the moment. I tried to simulate approval, but fell way short of the goal.

My Soul's Journey Through Some Of My Past Lives
Based Upon True Lives

"Oh no. You didn't. Did you?"

It was hard to contain my lack of enthusiasm. Sue and I were having way different reactions. I did not want to go to this nonsensical appointment.

"Don't you want to know? Aren't you curious?" she said, sipping her tea.

"Come on! It will be fun! Don't be such a bummer. It's my gift to you for letting me stay here."

I could think of other things that she could do for me. This certainly wasn't one of them. I had hoped to spend the day with Sue exploring the city. Maybe a museum or art exhibit. Seeing a past life regressionist? Uhm, no!

Sue was difficult to persuade. As for myself, I was so thrilled to have a friend to spend the day with, I finally just said, "Okay fine".

My Soul's Journey Through Some Of My Past Lives
Based Upon True Lives

The next thing I knew, we were on our way to the Village.

My Soul's Journey Through Some Of My Past Lives
Based Upon True Lives

Session Date: 9-25-15

~83~

Oversoul

We sit within all aspects of this energy as it explores the probabilities of gender. The idea of masculine/feminine often a component of understanding the nature of one's energy.

Not all universes embrace this perspective, however, the energies we look after are submerged in the inequality and quality of the male/female.

A great focus within a physical life, can render the energy void

Our focus is to aid in a more complete awareness of all aspects in multiple linear realities. By doing so, the soul/energy has an opportunity to make more complete, less edited, choices.

My Soul's Journey Through Some Of My Past Lives
Based Upon True Lives

In the instance of Mary, much of her self-deprecation in the current life is based upon other lives that were lacking in any sort of respect for her feminine qualities. Thus, her ability to free herself of that perceived judgement in parallel lives leaves her in an incompleteness in the one she is in.

Our hope by intervening through the current communication via email will prompt her to look past the current moment. So far, this has been stuck in a singular perspective that has left her stagnant.

It is necessary sometimes to prompt an aspect to look beyond their current circumstance. Should Mary expand her perspective on life experience, perhaps she will consider the totality of said experience. In that way, more growth may be available.

It is after all, the perspective of an aspect to expand in conjunction with all of its lives, not just one.

My Soul's Journey Through Some Of My Past Lives
Based Upon True Lives

Session Date: 10-03-15

~84~

Mary

The spartan waiting room had the faint aroma of one too many sweaty humans awaiting their appointment. My nostrils flared as we waited for this woman to allow us into her inner sanctum. At least it wasn't full of hocus pocus nonsense. Sue insisted this Dr. Kahn was a legitimate hypnotherapist with a degree in psychology. If she was truly successful, why did she dabble in this past life stuff? Did not make sense to me. Sue on the other hand was brimming with praise for the woman.

All I wanted was for it to be over with. To satisfy my friend and leave this behind. I merely was indulging my friend.

My Soul's Journey Through Some Of My Past Lives
Based Upon True Lives

The office door opened revealing an older woman. I was surprised at her frail demeanor. Her eyes were kind as she smiled at the two or us.

"Dr. Kahn! So good to see you!" gushed Sue. "I've brought my friend Mary. She needs to be regressed so she can discover her full self!"

I admit I was very embarrassed at the introduction. However, the presence of this woman was a soothing one. I felt better when she took my hand. Somehow, she felt oddly familiar.

Sue, of course, was already in her inner office ready to go. She was so excited to share this with me that I was compelled just to go along. Now it would be easier, for I rather liked Dr. Kahn.

The inner office was fragrant with flowers. Jasmine immediately came to mind.

"Why is it Jasmine?" said Dr. Kahn rather out of nowhere. I had not said anything out loud, but she had answered my question.

Dr. Kahn sat before us calmly while explaining the procedure of a past life regression. It did not seem like I would be a good candidate, but unwillingly I sat before her to be hypnotized. Or at least I was agreeable, not certain of any success.

Sue could barely contain herself. Sitting on the side sofa, she forced herself to be still. Hopefully this would go well, so she would stop prattling on about it so.

The sound of Dr. Kahn's voice was relaxing. Taking direction in this process was easier than I thought it would be. A feeling of calm enveloped me. Well at least that was a bonus.

My Soul's Journey Through Some Of My Past Lives
Based Upon True Lives

Session Date: 10-5-15

~85~

Mary

Soon there emerged a sensation that enveloped me like a soft warm blanket. I could still hear Dr. Kahn's voice, but it became distant as I began to focus upon a lamp that had a flame dancing in the breeze.

"What do you see?" asked Dr. Kahn from far away.

My voice sounded thin to me, as if I couldn't muster enough energy for the correct volume. I desperately wanted some tea to clear my throat. The walls were tapestry lined, not the sterile grey walls of Dr. Kahn's office.

My Soul's Journey Through Some Of My Past Lives
Based Upon True Lives

I considered being afraid, but found my interest superseded any reluctance. What was happening?

The voice kept asking what I saw. There were elegant decorations I was unfamiliar with. I could see my hands as they reached for a cup that would satisfy my urgent thirst. It was like warm tea. My lips so parched welcomed its moisture. Oh God! It was Jasmine tea. The smell and taste undeniable.

The voice kept asking me questions as the scenery changed to a stark room made of stone. My knees ached with cold as my feet shuffled to a destination unknown. Where was I?

A distant ringing of what sounded like a bell grabbed my attention. My skin felt the rough fabric of a long tunic of sorts.

The distant voice beckoned me to return, but where was I? The place looked like a church.... wait a minute..... it looks like nuns in the distance. What the hell was going on?

I turned my head and there was suddenly a busy street. Looked like a large metropolis, but where?

"Mary! Mary! On the count of 3 you will awake from your sleep. You will be refreshed and back in your own life.

"1 – 2 - 3!"

I felt myself lurch forward as if I had been tossed. With embarrassment, I managed to refocus upon Dr. Kahn. My friend.

Sue sat across the room in wide eyed amazement. A hundred questions came to mind, all at once.

What just happened?

Dr. Kahn snapped her fingers to enable a better focus. She did not look alarmed at all.

My Soul's Journey Through Some Of My Past Lives
Based Upon True Lives

"Well, you are a much better subject than either of us thought".

She smiled with enthusiasm, telling me that I had just skipped through several past lives without a lot of effort.

"You are such a good subject!" she declared.

As the room settled down I found myself quite intrigued with this whole past life stuff. The events leading up to this appointment were a bit unnerving, though. What was I to gain out of this?

There wasn't a lot of information that was presented, but I had definitely left this room, gone to a place unknown, unfamiliar, with ease. I wanted to know more.

*My Soul's Journey Through Some Of My Past Lives
Based Upon True Lives*

Session Date: 10-6-15

~86~

Mary

Evidently the opportunity was over, but I felt compelled to stay. What I had seen and felt was just the tip of the iceberg. The overwhelming feeling of desire filled me.

I did not want to beg, but I would have had she not nodded her head in agreement.

"I tell you what," she said. "Let's take a small break. Say, fifteen minutes? I have some calls to return, so I'll be right back. Both of you relax, and when return we will give it another try."

When she closed the door, Sue could barely contain herself.

My Soul's Journey Through Some Of My Past Lives
Based Upon True Lives

"Oh my God!" she exclaimed.

"You were great! Where did you go? It sounded fantastic!"

Sue was practically jumping out of her skin. I on the other hand, felt pensive. What did it mean? I wished Sue would just be quiet and let me think.

Sue rambled on, while I tried to relax. I so wanted to give it another try. I knew though, getting all excited would sabotage what we were trying to do. I smiled to myself that here I was doing a past life regression. Never would I have imagined it. All of the events this week seemed to lead to this very moment.

The door opened and Dr. Kahn came through.

"Well, let's begin again shall we?"

Sue sat down and I decided this time to lay down on the sofa. Somehow I felt I needed to relax more.

Dr. Kahn dimmed the lights and we began. I immediately felt light. I trusted a bit more this time as I closed my eyes. The lilt of the doctor's voice was soothing. She led me through a series of prompts. I could feel the confines of the room slip away. There was nothing but me in a large space. The hum of the electricity in the lamp became very loud. I wanted to open my eyes, but decided not to.

I was on a hammock of sorts with a cool breeze dancing across my brow. I could hear Dr. Kahn's voice become fainter and fainter. All that remained was me. A "me" I had never encountered before as these words came to my lips.

Session Date: 10-7-15

~87~

Mary

The voice was strong in my head. Undeniable thoughts, some long buried, others rising out of the ashes of other lives and places.

I can see images of Hasor. A slight slip of a girl on her wedding day to a man she did not know. A woman who in an effort for balance deciding to participate as a man in relationships. The vision was, and is, endless. There are more than I can count. An overwhelming energy should be present. Instead I felt a deep connection with this Hasor. Something of value would come from this connection. She was the beauty as I was not. Yet a sliver of awareness connected us without words. She reached out to me for a reason. I need to know why?

The swirl of energy diminished and the lull of Dr. Kahn's voice became louder. I was returning to be myself, Mary. Just Mary. I had value and a connection with something more than my perceived mundane life.

When I opened my eyes, Dr. Kahn was looking straight into my eyes.

"You must help me," I said softly.

"I will," she whispered.

The appointment was finished for now. Arrangements were made for a series of sessions. Sue was ecstatic, while wanting to be a part of it. Deep inside I knew this was personal. Funny how much things change in a week. Non-believer to Believer.

On the way home, we stopped for tea. Jasmine tea. Somehow it just felt right.

My Soul's Journey Through Some Of My Past Lives
Based Upon True Lives

Session Date: 10-12-10

~88~

Mary

My eyes are closed so that the light of the day makes no difference. I lose myself in thoughts of romance. A whiff of fragrance changes my thoughts to a moment that feels like fantasy but the vividness prevails and I succumb totally. I ride the wave of remembrance feeling as if all were still right here in my existence.

To become completely conscious now I have to let go of what was. The thought compelling but ultimately the answer is no.

"No. I cannot release what lingers in the crevices of my mind, or is it my soul?"

So profound, it has to be the latter.

My Soul's Journey Through Some Of My Past Lives
Based Upon True Lives

Fascinated, I reach into my heart knowing that what is now is only now. A piece of the puzzle that presents itself while I breathe the night air.

So many times I have done so. All seem like a blur until I pause enough to realize they all fit together in a mosaic created by the energy of myself.

I feel myself becoming more but the definition has so many layers. I often become confused.

Session Date: 10-26-10

~89~

Mary

"Am I Mary? Or am I this vixen of desire, intent upon reaching out to find a partner.

The zeal for that relationship fills my thoughts until I think I will explode.

Most of my friends find my behavior contradicting that which they know. For years I walked meekly among them practically a shadow of who I felt I was inside. I kept most of it tucked away so that they would still like me... their friendship important to me.

Mary.

Just plain Mary.

That was all they really understood. All of the other experiences I kept close to me, sharing only once in a while with a smirk upon my lips so that they would not guess the truth.

Since childhood these memories have plagued me. Vivid scenarios of a place that resembled Egypt. Well, maybe it *was* Egypt. I've never been able to determine for sure the location. I only remembered the dress and mannerisms of those I encountered.

Surely I, the Mary, never knew these people in this life. Gosh, it sounds so mysterious... this life. As if I have had others. See, here's where I become confused.

"Is it me or just a memory made up in fantasy? I don't know."

All that remains are the vivid pictures of another time and place. It sure isn't here. And in these places I look the same, but circumstances are very different, and so am I.

I used to be uncomfortable but I've outgrown that. Now I only wish to figure it out. To determine if it's just a dream or is it really me in another time.

"Wow, if it is?!"

I'm much more complex than I ever imagined.

My Soul's Journey Through Some Of My Past Lives
Based Upon True Lives

Session Date: 11-21-14

~90~

Oversoul

The interconnection of multiple life experience is often misinterpreted by those who can only view the current flow of life energy. If one can for a minute consider the multiplicity of the dramatics that surround the concepts of an eternal lesson plan, perhaps then the interweaving of life dramatics would make more sense to the average individual.

So far, the individual experiences are only intersecting mildly. In full swing, often the polar enactments blend in harmony to allow the soulful energy a broad perspective of what is to be learned.

My Soul's Journey Through Some Of My Past Lives
Based Upon True Lives

Session Date: 10-7-15

~91~

Oversoul

The aspects connecting was not preplanned, however, it was an enticing string of events. Perhaps there would be benefit in this communication. All seemed to be in agreement. The Sr. Ann would have to be guided out of the current belief system, along with Francine. Often the religious beliefs overlapped into inaccurate participations.

In the big perspective, all of the many aspects could be led to intersect while living through incarnate moments.

We are pleased Mary discovered her inner being while letting go of her self-deprecating self-beliefs.

As we have stated, this is but a slice of the pie. We hope to engage all of them further down their evolving paths.

It will be interesting to see what Mary ultimately discovers.

Session Date: 10-5-15

~92~

Epilogue

"What has been shared is a minor slice of the reincarnational process. Think of each one presented as a pinpoint reflection of the vast prism of aspects that each soul group provides.

To list them all in an endless fashion would ultimately prove confusing to those who read about the lives.

In this book we condensed the energy to give the sense and feel of the phases of participation and the perspective of the Oversoul as events unfolded.

The story obviously continues, however, at this time perhaps reflection is important.

HASOR

*My Soul's Journey Through Some Of My Past Lives
Based Upon True Lives*

You are all multidimensional beings having the experiences in and out of various time lines.

Expanding your awareness of your total energy was the guideline we followed.

Perhaps we will continue the story/stories at a later linear time...."

~HASOR

Appendix

Appendix

Warning: This appendix is only for those technical geeks and wonks interested in trance channeling like me who would be the type, for example, to read the notes by Robert Butts in the Seth Books written via Jane Roberts. If you do not know who Robert Butts and Jane Roberts are, you probably do not qualify as one who would enjoy reading further. So at least you have been warned:

Start by knowing that these sessions, both in-person and via writing, are extraordinary by any definition. There are about seven billion incarnated people here as of the publishing of this book. Even if there are a handful of individuals who are as naturally talented in terms of being a full body <u>open</u> deep trance channel, able to completely leave her physical form to allow various nonphysical beings to fully use that form physically to visit with us while she is out of body doing equally interesting things... well, I [Allen] am very fortunate given my interests in this material to have had at least hundreds of first hand in-person exchanges and question sessions with at least dozens of different nonphysical beings including those who have incarnated, and those who have not.

I personally do not care for the casual use of the term "walk-in" because there are so many levels and nuances involved in that. Probably most people think of it as a simple trade of a nonphysical being with a physical being who was going to "die" anyway, so why waste a perfectly good physical body?

However, so-called "walk-ins" have many levels, from a mere temporary blending of consciousness, even for a temporary single pivotal life moment, to a full blown exchange of beings regarding a physical form, and everything in-between The full blown form of it does come close to describing what April Crawford and those who temporarily trade places with her do.

However, even that is a considerable understatement, as those who come in, and assume total physical inhabitation, also, usually, retain a connection with the other side, including what most would deem to be the "psychic" abilities of reading energies, including all past lives of anyone who exists or who has ever existed physically, or otherwise.

It can be unnerving if one attempts to debate them for intellectual sport or knowledge, something I always engage in if for no other reason than to induce them to stay or to consider return visits. After all, given their vast choices of where they choose to be and focus, they always have other things to do. Thus my attempt at "intellectual bait".

The aspect of HASOR that I [Allen] talk with in full blown two way casual conversation is a being that because of her sophistication, physical and mental nuanced abilities and mere presence [Think Cleopatra level style and intellect], I considered for sure to be an Entity. However in a conversation with this particular aspect of HASOR (she simply goes by the name "Hasor", she surprised me by stating that she was not an Entity, but a personality (Aspect of an Entity) that enjoys having lots of physical incarnations, almost always as a female.

Appendix

She also stated specifically in answer to one of my questions, that she is not the Oversoul, although the aspects that wrote for this book are part of her, and are several of her many multiple physical incarnations. This Hasor, the one I visit with in-person via the Open Deep Trance Channel, also said that she has a good relationship with the Oversoul, but is quite an independent self-aware identity in her own right.

In an attempt to avoid continuing with my customary long winded discourse on what true full body open deep trance channeling actually is, fore it is very exciting, or to describe my many conversations with Hasor, and others, I will simply say as a matter of historical reference, that I first met Hasor in one of our "open invitation" nights after an outdoor evening visit with the Causal Plane Entity VERONICA.

Hasor and I hit it off, and after Hasor described a particularly interesting relationship she had with a historically well-known male figure in ancient Greece, somehow we agreed to do this book.

Appendix

Interestingly, that life in Greece is not included in this book! Perhaps in another volume. Hasor has teased that that particular relationship could take an entire book. I had spoken with that historically well-known male relationship of Hasor's on numerous occasions *before* ever meeting Hasor, and he has suggested that he may contribute to a future book.

As a further "tease", that now nonphysical being is one of only two Source Entities that I am aware of to ever physically incarnate fully as themselves (as opposed to creating aspects of themselves to incarnate physically.) If we can arrange such a book, I for one am excited.

For those with a specific interest in our work, contact me by email and I will answer specific questions. Those qualified to be one of our research and investment partners do have priority.

~Allen, Facilitator for April Crawford

About The Authors

HASOR

HASOR is the Oversoul to the incarnated Hasor, Mary, Clare, and Sister Ann, all of whom are authors of parts of this book in their own right as individuals.

All of them consider themselves to be the primary life, with the others being their "past" or multiple lives. Probably none of them are really aware of their Oversoul.

They all have been able to write their individual stories by temporarily assuming the physical form of the Open Deep Trance Channel, April Crawford. In addition, another aspect of Hasor has visited with me [Allen] on various occasions and was instrumental in starting the commitment to write this book, and no doubt participated in some of the narration.

About The Authors

All of the incarnated aspects are part of the Hasor I visited with (and still visit with). The Oversoul HASOR is separate an ultimately contains all of them... and much more.

April Crawford

April Crawford is an AMAZON Top 50 Best Selling Author across all book categories, and a Number One Best Selling Author in various related genres. April Crawford is also one of the world's most naturally talented and adept Full Body Open Deep Trance Channels and Spiritual Mediums. April and the Causal Plane Entity/Guide VERONICA have consulting clients in most countries of the world.

About The Authors

April Crawford's spiritual newsletter, *"Inner Whispers"*, is written by highly evolved nonphysical Entities and guides, primarily by VERONICA, and is read by tens of thousands of readers each week. It is available (free) at www.InnerWhispers.net

April currently lives in Los Angeles, California with her husband, Allen, and her many pets.

Additional Information

For more information about April Crawford, VERONICA, or about True Full Body Open Deep Trance Channeling: www.AprilCrawford.com

For the free spiritual newsletter *"Inner Whispers"*: www.InnerWhispers.net

To see VERONICA and April Crawford speaking, try www.InnerWhispersTV.com

About The Authors

For personal telephone or in-person consultations with VERONICA via April Crawford, Personal Appearances or Media Interviews with April Crawford and/or VERONICA, contact Allen at AprilReadings@aol.com

**

OTHER BOOKS

Written via

APRIL CRAWFORD

All books written via April Crawford are available from AMAZON via www.AprilCrawfordBooks.com

Dear VERONICA Book II: A Spirit Guide Answers 150 Letters

For more information:

www.DearVeronicaBook2.com

Available also for Kindle and Nook

"Inner Whispers": Messages From A Spirit Guide (Volume I)

Available also for Kindle and Nook

For more information:

www.InnerWhispersTheBook.com

"Inner Whispers": Messages From A Spirit Guide (Volume II)

Available also for Kindle and Nook

For more information:

www.InnerWhispersBookTwo.com

Other Books Written via April Crawford

"Inner Whispers": Messages From A Spirit Guide (Volume III)

Available also for Kindle and Nook

For more information:

www.InnerWhispersBookThree.com

"Parting Notes": A Connection With The Afterlife

Available also for Kindle and Nook

For more information: www.PartingNotes.com

"In The AfterLife":
A Chronicle Of Our Experiences On The Other Side

Available also for Kindle and Nook

Ashram Tang... a Story... and a Discovery

Available also for Kindle and Nook

www.AshramTang.com

Reflections of a Spiritual Astronaut: Book I

Available for Kindle and Nook

Reflections of a Spiritual Astronaut: Book II

Available for Kindle and Nook

Other Books Written via April Crawford

your life and its choices: THE RECIPE FOR ASCENTION TO ANOTHER PLANE "A" TO "Z"
By Ish and Osco (Spirit Guides) via April Crawford
Available for Kindle and Nook

Deep Trance Channeling Sessions: Special Edition No. 1
Available for Kindle and Nook

"Be bold when the opportunity presents itself..."

~VERONICA

Recommended Reading and Other Media

I) The Nature of Reality and Consciousness; Trance Channeling

By far and away, the Seth Books, written via trance channel Jane Roberts with notes from her husband Robert Butts:

Seth Speaks: The Eternal Validity of the Soul, Seth via Jane Roberts and Robert Butts

The Nature of Personal Reality: Specific, Practical Techniques for Solving Everyday Problems and Enriching the Life You Know, Seth via Jane Roberts and Robert Butts

The Nature of the Psyche: Its Human Expression (A Seth Book), Seth via Jane Roberts and Robert Butts

Recommended Reading And Other Media

Every other book written by Seth via Jane Roberts, including **The Private Sessions** and **The Early Sessions** series of Seth books.

II) <u>Spirituality and Consciousness</u>

The Seven Spiritual Laws of Success: A Practical Guide to the Fulfillment of Your Dreams, by Deepak Chopra

Your Erroneous Zones: Step-by-Step Advice for Escaping the Trap of Negative Thinking and Taking Control of Your Life, by Wayne Dyer

The Power of Now: A Guide to Spiritual Enlightenment, by Eckhart Tolle

Jonathan Livingston Seagull, by Richard Bach

Illusions: The Adventures of a Reluctant Messiah, by Richard Bach

Recommended Reading And Other Media

Super Soul Sunday, TV show (Oprah Winfrey Host, Oprah Winfrey Network)

(III) Manifesting, Law of Attraction, Like Attracts Like

The ***Seth Books*** written by the Entity Seth via trance channel Jane Roberts (see above).

Wishes Fulfilled: Mastering the Art of Manifesting, by Wayne Dyer

Ask and It Is Given: Learning to Manifest Your Desires, by Esther Hicks, Jerry Hicks, and Wayne Dyer (forward)

Creating Money: Attracting Abundance, by Sanaya Roman

The Secret by author Rhonda Byrne

(IV) Learning to Channel

Opening to Channel: How to Connect with Your Guide, by Sanaya Roman

Recommended Reading And Other Media

(V) Out of Body Experiences

Journeys Out of the Body, by Robert Monroe

Far Journeys, by Robert Monroe

The Monroe Institute, Learning Center

Leaving the Body, by Scott Rogo

Out-Of-Body Adventures, by Rick Stack

**(VI) Relay Mediums: Contact with
Friends and Relatives Who Have Crossed Over**

One Last Time, by John Edward

*Talking to Heaven: A Medium's Message of
Life After Death*, by James Van Praagh

Tim Braun, relay medium that we know personally,
www.TimBraun.net

Brian Hurst, relay medium that we know
personally, www.BrianHurst.com

Recommended Reading And Other Media

(VII) Reincarnation and Spirit Guides

The Oversoul Seven Trilogy: The Education of Oversoul Seven, The Further Education of Oversoul Seven, Oversoul Seven and the Museum of Time (Roberts, Jane), by Jane Roberts

(VIII) VIDEO

www.InnerWhispersTV.com

(IX) ONES TO WATCH

Sir Richard Branson:
A spiritual metaphysics thread running through him. May manifest itself more profoundly in coming times.

Paul Allen

If he ever gets past the physical technology limitations of his SETI radio wave communications box and realizes that interstellar distances hardly make same a choice vs. the simultaneous nature of consciousness as the medium, he may make some break throughs.

***

Made in the USA
San Bernardino, CA
19 November 2015